Samuel Grandjean

GENOVIEVA

A True Story

Eastern Europe Aid Association
Waynesboro, Pennsylvania

GEN

A range of mountains, wheat-covered plains, picturesque villages with rough roads—this is the beautiful country of Romania. In the fields are large flocks of sheep, and in the thick forests live wolves, and sometimes even bears.

Iași* is a pretty town in the northeast of the country. There, in a square not far from their home, three boys are talking. The old bench under the tree is a good place to meet. Oh, how many secrets that old wooden bench has heard! It is a good thing that it can keep secrets.

"I'm so tired," complains Iulian. "Today is Sunday. Why don't they let us rest? From nine in the morning till three in the afternoon we have to work. I think that's too much! In winter we have to shovel snow for hours. And now in this heat, we have to water corn fields with those little watering cans…"

"If only we had enough to eat. But what is there in the shops? Only dry bread and potatoes…"

"My mother had a hard time yesterday," adds Petru. "She stood in line at the butcher shop

* Pronounced *Yash*.

2.

OVIEVA

A True Story

from four o'clock in the morning. When her turn came to be served there was nothing left. She came home empty-handed. And that wasn't the first time!"

"Look!" interrupts Cornel. "There's Genovieva. Don't say a word!"

Genovieva is one of their classmates. She approaches them with a smile.

"Hello!"

Silence.

"Hello!" repeats Genovieva in surprise.

"Listen," says Cornel. "You know very well we are not allowed to talk to you. Get away from here! If you stay with us, you will get us into trouble."

"But… what have I done?"

"Nothing. It's… because of your parents. Leave us alone now, Genovieva!"

The little girl goes away thoughtful. She sits down all by herself at a distance.

But my parents are so nice, she says to herself with a sigh. *So, I dare not talk to my classmates any more. At school during recess it's just as bad. I have to stay on a bench all by myself, with my hands behind my back.*

Is Genovieva badly behaved at school? Certainly not! Then why do they treat her like that? Is she naughty or impolite? No, she is just an ordinary child. But there must be a reason for it. A child wouldn't be treated that way for nothing. "It's because of your parents…" said Cornel. So who are these parents of hers? Are they bad people? Do they steal?

No, her parents are just… Christians. What lies are spread about believers! They are called "dangerous people you can't trust!" Genovieva's parents know all about it. But they cannot give up what they have found in the Bible. Should they pretend they don't know Jesus Christ? Never! He has given them peace, joy and a sense of security. After all, what does it matter if they are ridiculed? They have found so much in Him!

It's true, we are poor, sighs the little girl, as she makes her way home. *And yet my parents are so nice!*

She is now in front of their little house. It has only one floor, but they are content with that. It is true that her father is an inspector of bridges. But, because he is a Christian, he is paid very little.

Their house is on a quiet street in the northern part of the city. It is in an area near the Russian border. But, whatever are those strange buildings across the street? And what is that man doing on the roof? We'll soon find out!

3

Songs Cross the Street

"Come, children, let's sing!" says their father one day.

"Oh yes, Dad!" shout the children. "Will you play your violin?"

"Yes, of course. I've just tuned it."

"Hurrah! It is going to be a nice concert."

"Come on, then," repeats Father. "Are you all ready? We'll begin with a folk song. How about one of those beautiful Romanian tunes?"

The little choir sings joyfully. It is nice to be together as a family. There, no one criticizes you for believing in God.

Meanwhile, Mother prepares the evening meal. The kitchen is simple, with a small wood-burning stove. She makes a good potato soup, and soon no one will be hungry any longer.

That's all there is for supper.

This morning, like many other mornings, she waited for hours in long lines at the shops. But all she could find was stale bread and potatoes...

"Now," continues Father, "I am going to teach you a nice new song. First of all I'll play the tune... Listen to the words. Do you like it? It is about God, our Creator."

"But Dad," interrupts eight-year-old Costică, "our teacher tells us every morning that there is no God."

"Oh, the poor lady! She doesn't know God. I'm sure she has never read the Bible."

"Oh, Dad," exclaims Genovieva suddenly, "someone's screaming again. Another prisoner is being beaten."

A prisoner? Yes, that's right. Just across the street from their house is a prison. Some are there simply because they are Christians. That is what goes on in this country. There is much suffering in many families.

"Oh, Dad, I have an idea," says Genovieva one day. "You know the prisoners come out in the yard every day before they go to work. Let's go in the garden and sing for them right then. We sing so well! We could begin with folk songs and then... continue with a Christian song. That might encourage them, don't you think?"

"Yes, Genovieva, that's a very good idea."

So now our "choir" stands in the garden. Father takes his violin. What a lovely concert! They all stand with their backs to the road. It looks as if they are playing for someone in their house. But the music and words can easily cross the street. What a joy it is for the children to sing! And how their singing touches the hearts of the prisoners!

One day there is a knock at the door. Who is this lady? Her face is half hidden by a woollen shawl.

"Cătălina!" exclaims Mother, giving her a hug. "Come in quickly. We've been thinking a lot about you."

"Thank you. I need that. It's hard to be suddenly without a husband, especially with four children at home."

"Tell us about it, Cătălina. What happened?"

"One of my husband's co-workers was interested in the Bible. He didn't have one, so Nicolae promised to lend him his. The other day, after work, he gave it to him..."

"But a supervisor noticed," continues Cătălina, "and he informed the police at once. They

treated Nicolae very roughly and took him away. I wonder which prison they put him in, and how long they'll keep him there?"

Poor Cătălina! In order to get to Genovieva's parents' house she had to travel right to the north of the town. She knew that she would find their house at the end of a quiet street—the last house on the left. To the right—no, she didn't dare to look in that direction. Besides, it is forbidden. A large sign warns passers-by in several languages: "Entrance Forbidden!" The local people know what that means: Don't stop here! Keep going! Don't look this way! And above all, don't take photographs!

Who is behind those walls? Nicolae perhaps, or other men they call "dangerous." When they arrest them, this is what they tell them:

"We warned you not to poison people with your Christian ideas. But you did not listen, and now you have to pay dearly for your disobedience."

"Wait a minute, Cătălina," suggests Genovieva. "I've finished my homework. I'll stand at the window and if I see anything, I'll call you. But don't let anyone see you!"

She goes to the window to watch. In front of the window is an orchard. The two apple trees spread their branches apart so that she can see the other side of the street. There is a wall, and behind it is a low tower. There is someone on its concrete roof. It is a soldier walking up and down with a machine-gun. Every now and then he makes a sign to his comrade, who is keeping watch at the other tower.

The dismal buildings can be seen through the iron bars on top of the wall. How many times Genovieva has watched them from that window! She has often seen the prisoners coming out through the big gate, then going to cut wood in the nearby park. There is always a guard going ahead of them, and another following them, with two large Alsatian dogs. Woe to the one who would try to escape!

No, Cătălina couldn't catch a glimpse of her husband. But after a week in prison, Nicolae was released. He determined to be even more careful in the future.

Genovieva is doing well at school and dreams of becoming a... Ah, but we mustn't rush ahead!

What "surprises" are in store for her?

The Teacher's Questions

"Time to get up, children!" says Mother. "Get washed quickly and come for breakfast. Then it will be time for school."

The happy home is a hive of activity. Already Father is at his job.

Now the five children are round the table, each with a bowl of hot chocolate. Teodor's little face is still sleepy. He is the youngest and is only six years old.

"There… everyone have a slice of bread," says Mother, putting a little tray of bread on the table.

"Mom, why don't we ever have butter and jam on the bread any more?" asks Costică.

He is eight.

"Butter costs too much, and it's hard to find in the shops."

"But do you think we'll ever have any again?"

"I don't know, my dear, but let's be thankful for the little we still have."

"Butter or no butter, when you're hungry everything tastes good," interrupts Genovieva. "I'm very hungry this morning."

"Those who go to school get ready now," says Mother. "The mornings are starting to get cold. Don't forget your thick sweaters, and your hat, Lola."

Winter is indeed approaching. Some days the thermometer goes way down. Then everything freezes solid. You can't escape the cold anywhere, whether at home or at school.

Little Teodor is still at home. He doesn't mind at all. As for Genovieva, in the mornings she does her homework. In the afternoons she has to be at school, sometimes till eight o'clock at night. It is dark by the time she gets back.

Genovieva works very hard at school. She is one of forty children in her class. This afternoon, after the math and reading class, it is the recess. She has become used to spending twenty minutes sitting on a bench away from her classmates. Now it is time for classes to start again. But not as usual.

"Close your books," says the teacher. "Each one of you in turn is to stand up and answer my questions. I will start with you, Ghiocel. Tell me… have you ever seen a Bible?"

"No, Sir," replies the little boy.

"And has anyone ever told you about it?" asks the teacher.

"No, Sir. I don't know what it is."

"Very well. Now your turn, Rodica…"

And each child is asked the same questions.

When it comes to Genovieva's turn, she remembers her father's advice: "If you will ever have to answer difficult questions, always tell the truth."

"Yes, Sir. We have a Bible at home. My parents have often told me stories from it. I like the ones about Daniel, and Joseph, and especially about the Lord Jesus…"

"Sit down," says the teacher, visibly upset. "Enough of that!"

Genovieva's parents know that the teachers have to follow certain instructions: "Tell the children that God does not exist. If you have Christian pupils, give them bad marks. Humiliate them, ridicule them, punish them in front of the whole class. And, even if he deserves it, never give a prize to a child from a Christian family."

At the end of the day, the results of an examination will be given out. All the children are waiting impatiently to hear their name and their mark.

"Pavel!" begins the teacher. "Quite good, but there were a few mistakes. There is still room for improvement. Even so you got an eight. Carmen! Very good, apart from two small mistakes. A ten for you. Well done!"

And the list continues…

"Genovieva!" says the teacher suddenly. "You did very well too. There is no mistake. You got a five, and you know why."

"It's because she's a Christian," someone whispers in the class.

Yes, that is indeed the reason.

On their way out, all her classmates laugh at Genovieva. Oh, how that hurts! The little girl can't wait to get home, to be together with her family where she is happy.

Over the meal Genovieva tells them what happened…

"I understand, my dear," says her mother lovingly.

"But it's not fair," adds Dionisie, her elder brother.

"Of course not," sighs Mother. "But we are not the only ones to go through such trials. Listen to what a friend told me the other day:

"'In our town,' she said, 'we have a friend, Daniel, who is a Christian. He is only eleven. One Monday, in front of the whole class, the teacher asked him, "Why didn't you come to the *Pioneers** meeting yesterday morning?" Daniel answered, "Because on Sunday mornings I go to church with my parents." Stirred up by the teacher, all the pupils started to laugh. The teacher even had to ask them to stop. Then he asked Daniel, "Do you really believe in God…? Can you show us the way Christians pray? Go on, recite a prayer for us," the teacher added with a laugh. Daniel put his head down, his hands together, closed his eyes and began to pray: "Lord Jesus, thank You for loving and saving me, by giving Your life for me. Please save my classmates and my teacher too. Amen." The teacher was very embarrassed. As a punishment, Daniel was made to stand in a corner.'"

"Like Daniel in the Bible," says Genovieva, "he was faithful to God. Good for him!"

"And God will bless him, I'm sure," adds Mother. "At the end of the school year, some children are even deprived of prizes they deserved because they are Christians. But they will certainly win another prize which God will give them. And no one will be able to take that reward away from them."

* The Communist youth organization.

A Strange Present

"Oh, no, Genovieva!" protests little Teodor. "Are you going away again? But I wanted to play with you. You know... I hide under the bed, and you look for me. Or we could have a pillow fight..."

"Oh, I know you, little joker!" answers Genovieva. "You will be able to play with Costică. I have to go to school."

"But it's Sunday today. There is no school."

"I know it's Sunday, Teodor. But, without asking my opinion, they chose me as the president of the *Pioneers*. No more free Sundays!"

"But what are you going to do?"

"All sorts of things. First I have to prepare the activities class. Every room has to be swept. Then I have to arrange some flowers..."

"And after that will you come back?" he asks again.

"Not that soon. Some soldiers are coming to school this morning. They will attend the swearing-in ceremony of the new *Young Pioneers*. I will have to take the register, take notes, and start the songs. But this afternoon I will be home. Then I will have to write up a report of the long morning."

"And after that, can we…?"

"After, after… Quick, I have to go! I'll be late! I have to hurry now."

After kissing her little brother, Genovieva sets off as fast as she can. She has a twenty-five-minute walk. She wears her school uniform, as she does all week. It is a sort of blue pinafore dress. A strip of material is pinned to the left sleeve. Two numbers stand out in bright yellow. The first is the number of the school, and the second is Genovieva's number. Each pupil has to wear this distinguishing mark on his sleeve whenever he goes out. And if he wears a coat, this identifying strip has to be fixed on the sleeve.

This Sunday morning at church, Father will lead the choir. At school, Genovieva will listen to lectures which don't interest her. At home, the two small brothers will wait with their big sister, Aurora.

And what about Dionisie, the eldest brother? He is old enough to go to church with his parents.

Meanwhile, somewhere in the country of Romania, a prison door opens to admit someone. Then it closes behind him…

The new prisoner is put into a cell with Christians. Their only crime is preaching the Gospel.

Looking carefully at the newcomer, some of them recognize him. There is no doubt about it. He is a former police officer. Several believers have been arrested and interrogated by this man.

"What did you do to end up here?" they ask him.

Then the new prisoner begins to tell his story:

"Not very long ago, a little twelve-year-old boy came into my office. He had a flower in his hand. I was surprised to see him. So I asked him why he had come. 'Today is my mother's birthday,' he replied, 'and I love her very much. Each year I give her a flower as a present. But…' He hesitated a moment.

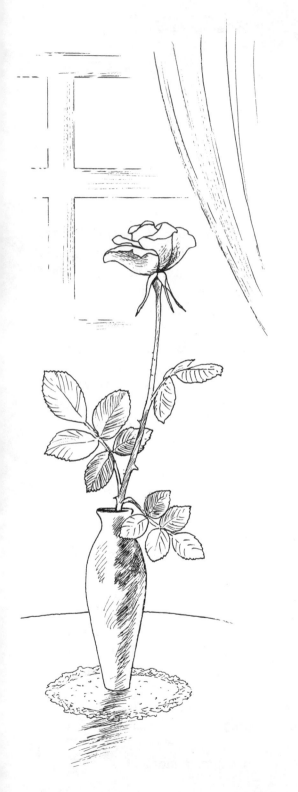

"Then he continued, 'But you arrested my mom and dad because they are Christians and took them away. Now, I have no one to give this flower to. So, give it to your wife! Tell her that I love you anyway, and tell her about Jesus Christ.' And the little boy gave me the flower. I was moved to the bottom of my heart. With tears in my eyes, I gave this boy a hug and promised him that I would never persecute Christians again. Since that day I have turned to God. I refused to arrest and interrogate believers. Then I myself was arrested and condemned as a Christian."

Hearing that, the prisoners thank the Lord for touching and saving one more soul, and for using a boy of twelve who was deprived of his parents.

In the Bible we read: "Remember those in prison as if you were their fellow-prisoners" (Hebrews chapter 13, verse 3).

That is why we must pray for our persecuted brothers and sisters and do all we can to help them.

A Very Difficult Decision

"You'll see, Genovieva," said her mother, "if you try very hard, you will pass your entrance exams for higher education."

She was right. Intelligent and hard-working, Genovieva was successful.

The situation in the country is not getting any better. Times are difficult, especially for the Christians. But the months and years go by just the same.

One nice day in June…

"Good," says a secretary at the university. "I have your family name… What is your first name?"

"Genovieva," replies a charming girl with a pretty face.

Then a photo is stapled to the registration paper.

"Fine!" says the secretary. "Your file is complete. We will see you at the beginning of September, when classes begin."

So Genovieva is a new university student. She is enthusiastic about her studies. Foreign literature, the history of a language and those who speak it, translation—everything interests her. But sometimes, Genovieva seems far away, deeply absorbed in her thoughts.

It's true, she says to herself, *my parents are Christians. That caused me a lot of mocking at school. Some believers are in prison because of their faith. But… what about me? Am I really a Christian? I read in the Bible: "By faith we have peace with God." Do I have this peace in my heart? I don't know. Sometimes I think I'm even afraid of being a real Christian.*

When she can, the young student goes to church with her parents. Like so many others, she has respect for the Bible. But, has she ever asked Jesus Christ to forgive her sins? No, not yet. The fact is that people have always treated her as a Christian, without her really being one.

Genovieva is now a brilliant student. She is so gifted, especially in English, that she could become a translator, an interpreter, or perhaps a teacher. But a few weeks ago, all the teachers who refused to teach atheism were dismissed from their jobs. It is more and more difficult to be a Christian. All the time you risk falling into a trap and having serious problems.

"Listen, let's be friends," Vanda suggests one day. She is a fellow student. "I would like you to give me a little help. You are so good at English!"

"Certainly!" replies Genovieva.

The two students start to meet regularly outside of classes. But soon Genovieva feels a certain awkwardness in Vanda's company. Why does her "friend" always want to talk about certain delicate subjects? Why does she insist so much on knowing whether Genovieva goes to Christian meetings, whether she has a part in them, and who the responsible person is?

Genovieva is very cautious. And rightly so. What does she discover one morning? Vanda is the daughter of the chief of the secret police, the man who does most to oppose the believers.

But the young student doesn't allow herself to be caught in a trap.

One day, though, she suddenly finds herself in a very embarrassing situation. We shall see why…

There is a knock at the door. Two gentlemen are standing at the

entrance of the family home. Genovieva immediately recognizes her pastor. The other visitor is unknown to her.

"Oh, Mr Marcu! Do come in! How nice to see you!" says Mother.

"I'm glad to see you, too. And I am delighted to find Genovieva here, as I have come to ask for her help."

"Really?" exclaims the young student, somewhat surprised.

"Let me introduce you to a Danish missionary who is visiting Romania," explains the pastor. "Unfortunately he doesn't speak our language. But he knows English very well. You can guess what I want, Genovieva."

"I don't understand, Mr Marcu."

"Then let me explain. It is rare to have a visitor from abroad. We must make the most of it and organize a meeting with the brothers and sisters. This servant of God will be able to encourage us all. And I am sure everyone will go away with a great blessing. I don't speak English. But you, Genovieva, are very good at it. So, would you agree to translate for our friend?"

Genovieva is dumbfounded.

"But, Mr Marcu, as you know… no, I really can't. Put yourself in my position. At university," she explains, "I am already watched by Vanda. If it becomes known that I did this translation, I would risk being expelled from university. My entire future is at stake."

"I understand, Genovieva, but it would really help us *so* much. We have no one else to translate… and you know, the eternal future of many may depend on this evening. Think about it, Genovieva. Please, do that for God and for me. Will you give me your answer by this time tomorrow? I'll come round to know your decision."

What a dilemma for the poor student! What should she do? After all, if she translates for this missionary, people won't necessarily know… But if they find out, it could be catastrophic for Genovieva. How hard it is to take a big decision alone!

The hours go by. Soon Mr Marcu will come for his answer. Genovieva wouldn't want to cause trouble for him. Oh, if only she could know the future! Then she could decide, bearing in mind what would happen later…

She has made up her mind. Without her suspecting anything, her entire future will depend on this choice.

A Very Great Day

"This way," someone whispers in the dark. "Look, you can see the walls of the prison. The house is opposite… Yes, there it is."

"Be sure to knock gently."

The door opens…

"Come in, quickly!" whispers a young man.

The door closes behind them.

It is almost nine o'clock in the evening. It got dark a long time ago. Already the town seems to be asleep. But what is happening in that house at the end of the road? Let's try to guess…

"Good evening, Smaranda! Good evening, Ioan! We were expecting you. Welcome! Others are still to come… There, someone else is knocking."

"Oh, it's Jănică! Come in, quickly! How are you?"

"Very well. What a good idea to have this home meeting tonight!"

"We really have to make the most of it. It's very

16

seldom we have visitors, and they are such a blessing!"

Christian meetings in homes are not authorized. You can understand why these people arrive so cautiously. There are about twenty present this evening.

The Danish preacher sits down at the family table. A girl takes her place beside him. It is Genovieva. He will speak in English, and she will translate for him.

"Dear friends," says the foreigner, "it's a great joy for me to spend this evening with you."

"Dear friends," repeats Genovieva in her beautiful Romanian. "I am glad to be with you this evening."

It is a good exercise for the young student. She has to concentrate, understand the exact meaning of each sentence, then faithfully repeat it in her mother tongue. Of all those present, she is the one who will have to listen most attentively.

"I love all the Christians in the world," the speaker is saying now, "but I have a special affection for those who are persecuted for their faith. If I could give my life for my brothers in Romania, I would do it…"

Genovieva is very touched as she translates that. But the preacher is already going on. "But that wouldn't be of much value. What do we read in the Gospel of John, chapter 15, verse 13?"

The Danish preacher turns over the pages of his New Testament. Genovieva does the same. Soon, in her turn, she reads: "Greater love has no one than this, that a man lay down his life for his friends."

"Who said that?" continues the speaker. "Jesus Christ Himself. He calls us His friends. He gave His life for you who listen, for me who speak to you, and for the girl who is translating. He died on a cross because of our sins. We can know that in our mind, with no change in our life. But we can also accept it with all our heart. Then we receive the forgiveness of sins and the certainty of going to heaven one day. A new life begins. Yes, we become new creatures. This evening, dear Romanian friends, I would like to be sure that you have accepted God's forgiveness. Whether or not we suffer mockery, loneliness, or persecution, what counts is to get to heaven one day… To be shut out is a very serious matter, for then it will be too late."

The speaker continues to speak. Genovieva continues to translate...

"The cross—that's how much Jesus loved us! Do you understand? Don't respond to me, but to Him. Now I will be quiet, so that you can speak to Him. Yes, you can do it right now."

The Danish preacher stops speaking. So does the translator. Never up to now has she felt such a need to speak to her God. Christians parents are fine, but that is no longer enough for her. She too wants to be a real Christian. She has understood. Jesus Christ is waiting for an answer. Then, without anyone hearing, from the depths of her heart, she gives Him her response: *Save me, Lord Jesus! Forgive my sins. Make me a new creature, and be my Guide in life.*

Without anyone hearing…? But someone has just heard. Who? Jesus Christ, the Savior.

So, for Genovieva, a simple evening of translation became the evening of the greatest encounter of her life.

Next morning the young student will wake up as usual. The color of her eyes will not have changed, nor the family home. And yet, from this day on everything will be different. From now on Jesus is her personal Savior. Genovieva will certainly continue to be ridiculed for being a Christian. She may even be persecuted. But at least she will know the One for Whom she is suffering.

An Unpleasant Surprise

At the family table, Genovieva is talking with her brother.

"Listen, Teodor! This Christian brother from Denmark is in our country for a few weeks. When translating for him the other evening I understood, and invited Jesus Christ into my life. I am so happy! This preacher wants to speak to the people in the neighboring villages. He needs someone to translate from English into Romanian. I am going to go along to be of service to him."

"I understand, Genovieva, and I admire you for that. But you are taking great risks. The secret police are everywhere. Think of Cătălin's father. He talked about God in public, and now he's in prison."

"I know," sighs Genovieva. "Such sad things are happening in

19

our country! But we believers who have the courage must do *something* even so."

"You certainly have changed, Genovieva!" says Teodor. "Remember how hesitant you were to translate for this brother when he came to our house? You were afraid you would have problems at university. And now you have the courage to go into these villages. Aren't you afraid any more?"

"No, my fear has gone! Since that evening, many things have changed in my life. I know that my sins are forgiven. The Bible tells me that, and it does me good. But there's something else I understand too."

"What? Quick, tell me…"

"At school they always pointed at me and called me 'the Christian girl.' I wasn't really one, as I hadn't then accepted Jesus as my Savior. But I found those mockings terrible. I was always afraid of them. Now everything is different. I will certainly have even more problems because I am a believer. But at least I will know the One I am suffering for, and that will help me."

"I am proud of you, Genovieva," Teodor hastens to add. "You know, I too met the Lord that evening. I know He will guide my life too."

With those words Teodor comes and sits down close to his sister. He has an idea…

"Genovieva, how about me going with you? We have a few days vacation and no one would know except for our family, of course. Didn't you say that this Christian man from Denmark is looking for some young people to go with him? You would do

the translation, and I would be ready to do anything, as you know. I could also sing and play the guitar…"

"Good idea! And I wouldn't be on my own. It would be much better for both of us to go. We must talk to Dad and Mom about it."

"Wonderful!" says Father immediately. "Many young people get bored or waste their time during the holidays. For you two, at least, it will be an enriching and useful experience. May God protect you as you go! But be careful, because the police are everywhere."

Taking a few things in a bag, very early the next morning the brother and sister go to the station and take a local train. A few hours later, they meet the preacher at the designated village. That evening, at the home of a Christian couple, many come to hear the Gospel.

Everyone appreciates Genovieva's translation. The young student puts all her heart and soul into it.

A little later the brother and sister go to bed on two mattresses spread on the floor in an attic. But the night will be short. In a few hours someone will come to wake them up. Why so early?

They will take advantage of the darkness to accompany the preacher to another village. In full daylight the little group would risk attracting too much attention. They have to be wise. But what a joy to be able to serve God!

Time passes too quickly on holiday. Soon classes at school and university will start again. Genovieva and her brother have to think about going home. There is a train leaving at four o'clock in the morning that will take them back into the city.

They are not the only ones at the little village station. As every day, some laborers are already on their way to work. But can you see that man with the black hat? He is in the same car and is keeping a close eye on our two young friends. Who is he? The other passengers don't seem to know him.

When the train arrives at its destination, the man with the black hat quickly gets up. He wants to be the first to get off. He seems to have a friend waiting for him on the platform. Indeed, they make a discreet little sign to each other…

The brother and sister make their way out of the station. So do the two men. The square is already bustling with activity as the morning begins. Teodor and Genovieva take a little street. They are followed into it…

Silently the two men catch up with them. One of them grabs the boy's arm with one hand, and shows a card with the other.

In surprise, Teodor looks at the face, then at the card. Two words are enough for him to understand: "Secret police."

"Where are you going, you two?"

"We're going home."

"And where are you coming from?"

"From a nearby village. We were staying with some friends for the holidays…"

"Follow us!" says the plainclothes officer.

"But…" protests Teodor.

"We'll leave explanations till later," replies the policeman sternly. "Come this way please!"

It is the first time that Genovieva and her brother have been arrested. Where are they being taken? And what is going to happen to them? They go without knowing…

In a side street, a car is waiting for them. They are forced to get in. They set off for the headquarters of the *Securitate.*[*] All Genovieva and Teodor can do is exchange a few anxious glances.

Soon the car enters a yard. A gate closes behind them. They have arrived. After climbing a few steps, they come to a long corridor. They take Genovieva to one room and her brother to another. The interrogation begins.

The session will last three long hours, and all the time they will be asked ques-

---

[*] The dreaded Romanian secret police.

tions like these:

"Whose home were you in? What did you do there? What did you talk about with your friends? Did you receive Bibles at home? Did you take any to your friends?"

In both rooms they give wise answers, and the policemen find that exasperating. Fortunately, Genovieva and her brother are not beaten. But they are severely threatened:

"You are not allowed to meet in the homes of Christians, or to meet with foreigners. You should know that, and you would do well to tell the others too."

But the policeman goes further:

"From now on we are going to keep a close watch on both of you."

"And if you don't want to have serious problems," adds the other officer, "try to remember what you are told. All right?"

"All right!"

"Now we will take you home. And we will soon know if you are hiding Bibles."

Then, turning to his colleague, the officer takes his revolver from his pocket.

"Have you got yours?" he asks.

"Yes," the other one replies, showing his weapon. "It's loaded."

They try hard to intimidate the two young Christians.

"All right, let's go! Get into the car!"

At last they are on the road and soon arrive home.

When the poor parents see their children escorted by three *Securitate* officers, their worry turns to fear.

While one officer keeps the family under guard, the other two carry out a systematic search of the house. Ah! If they can put their hands on a load of Bibles, they will have a very good reason for putting the parents in prison.

For more than two hours all the cupboards are examined. Even a mattress is ripped open. But fortunately the policemen don't find anything.

What a relief when at last they decide to leave!

"Take courage!" says Father. "Our God is almighty. He has promised to be our shield. Will He not do what He has said?"

A
Terrible
Blow

A few weeks have gone by since those events. Classes have started again after the holidays. Genovieva works hard, not only in English, but in all her other subjects.

This morning she goes to the university. There she has to take an oral examination, for which she has prepared very seriously. It concerns political doctrine, a compulsory subject for all students.

Genovieva knows many things, but one thing she doesn't know. The professor who teaches this subject at the university is at the same time a high-ranking *Securitate* officer. He has already been informed about her arrest.

In the entrance hall, outside the examination room, the students are waiting their turn. All morning is taken up with exams. When the door opens, the next student can go in and appear before the examiners. But first he must stop at a long table. There is a row of several envelopes on it, each containing a question. He takes three, and will be able to answer whichever one he chooses.

It is Genovieva's turn. She comes up to the big table and she grabs an envelope… then a second… then a third. But she is very surprised, because she finds the same question in each envelope: "What is meant by atheism according to its founder?"

Well, I don't have a choice, she says to herself. *But it doesn't matter. I worked hard enough on that subject. I can answer without hesitation.*

So Genovieva begins her answer. But suddenly the professor interrupts her:

"Please tell us what *you* think of atheism!"

Atheism denies the existence of God, but Genovieva has other convictions. Suddenly she is being asked what *she* thinks. But, that's not the question on the paper. Might this be a trap set for her?

"Excuse me, Professor," the student says very politely. "The question isn't what *I* think of atheism, but what the one who founded it thought of it."

"I know what I am asking," replies the examiner dryly.

Genovieva keeps quiet. But the professor gets angry.

"We know all about what you have been doing during your holidays. You had time to go away for four days in the country with your brother. It would have been more intelligent to prepare yourself a little better for such important exams. You have just failed miserably! You can go."

Genovieva is overwhelmed. She knew her subject well. They certainly wanted her to fail this exam. Whatever can she do?

After a long talk with her parents, Genovieva requests an interview with the director of the university. This man has always been very friendly. He will certainly be able to understand the situation, give some advice, or even intervene.

The director receives the student, but he seems very annoyed. Finally he says:

"I received some information about you concerning your activities outside the university. It seems that you have been playing the part of a translator in secret Christian meetings."

"That's right, Sir, but during the holidays."

Genovieva's heart is beating very fast. For a fraction of a second, a crowd of images flash into her mind: The evening at home when she translated for the first time. Then the request to visit some villages. The trip with Teodor, the clear preaching of the Gospel, the joy of translating for such attentive people. Coming home, being arrested, and the endless interrogation in the *Securitate* building…

"As a result," continues the director, "I see no other alternative than to expel you from the university. I am very sorry, for you are a brilliant student, especially at English. I must inform you that all access to other higher education is closed to you in the future. But, if you wish, in two years' time you will be able to take the university examinations again."

What a blow for Genovieva! When she came into this building a moment ago, she had no idea that it would be for the last time.

"This is news that will change my future," she tells her father when she gets home. "Out of love for my Savior, I did those translations. And now I have to give up my studies… What am I going to do?"

"Listen, Genovieva," her father says after a long silence. "Out of love for you, Jesus gave up the glory of heaven when He came to earth. Out of love for you, Jesus didn't shrink from the sufferings of the cross. Out of love for you, I'm sure that He will take care of you, and that He will allow your life to be even more useful for Him. Let's pray together! Let's ask Him to accomplish His plans for you, even if the way He leads you isn't the one you would have chosen. Never forget what God said: 'I know the plans I have for you, plans to prosper you and not to harm you, plans to give you hope and a future. Then you will call upon Me and come and pray to Me, and I will listen to you.' God does what He promises, Genovieva."

Caught in a Trap

While she was studying, everything went quite well for Genovieva. But since she was expelled from university, she has been under a threat.

Here, she says to herself, *the law forbids being unemployed. I must quickly find a job. Otherwise I risk being put in a labor camp. I would rather sweep the streets.*

Then she gets busy, knocking every day at several doors. She is ready to do anything. Each time, she has to fill out a questionnaire, and everywhere she hears:

"You will have an answer in two or three days."

She waits hopefully. But when she does get an answer, it is always no. So what's going on? Finally she understands. Before employing someone, they get information. And they discover Genovieva's name on a list of people who have had problems with the police. Then the decision is quickly made:

"We certainly won't employ that girl. We will have problems

with the *Securitate*."

In vain Genovieva goes from one place to another. Everywhere it is the same.

Of course, she is not idle at home. In a large family there is no lack of housework—especially when the home is open to other believers. At least once a week, one of them comes to spend the evening with Genovieva's parents. His name is Gheorghe. He is a former teacher, and a committed Christian. For eleven years he was imprisoned because of his faith. But he remained steadfast. Genovieva has a high regard for him.

"It's strange," says Father one evening. "Our dear friend Gheorghe didn't come, and we were expecting him for the meal…"

Soon the family learns with dismay that this man has just been interned in a psychiatric hospital. In some countries—and Romania is one of them—such institutions are really prisons for many Christians.

"We can't leave our friend all alone in that hospital," exclaims Genovieva. "Tomorrow I am going to visit him."

And off she goes, taking some food which this brother will certainly appreciate.

Acting quite naturally, she presents herself at the entrance of the hospital…

"You have a visitor, Gheorghe," the former teacher soon hears.

He looks towards the corridor in surprise…

"Oh, Genovieva!" the believer suddenly exclaims. "What a joy to see you! Yes, I am very well."

However, he takes the girl's arm, and adds in a low voice:

"Come, I'll tell you what happened to me…"

Wisely, Genovieva doesn't stay long. But she makes up her mind to come back. Really, this respected believer is imprisoned there, isn't he? And doesn't it say in the Bible: "Remember those in prison"?

Time goes by. Genovieva continues to look for work. But it is a lost cause. There is nothing for her. Oh, how happy she would be to return to her studies!

"Listen!" a former university friend tells her one day. "Perhaps you do have a chance. A medical certificate could resolve everything. If you can prove that for health reasons you needed more time than others to prepare, you will be admitted for a new examination session.

"I have an uncle who is a doctor at the psychiatric hospital," the student explains. "That is where this certificate can be obtained."

"The psychiatric hospital? I know the place... I visited a friend of my parents there."

"Then go and introduce yourself to my uncle. It's bound to work."

For a long time Genovieva turns it over in her mind. This is a difficult step to take, but she would do anything to straighten out her situation.

Well, yes, she decides at last, *I am going to try to get this certificate.*

As a precaution, she goes to the hospital with her sister Aurora. What will the result of this consultation be? Oh, if only she knew all that was in store for her!

From the start, things don't go quite as she had thought.

"You will have to spend the night here," she hears. "The doctor cannot see you today. It is very important that you are 'under observation' for a few hours before this appointment."

"Then I will stay," Genovieva resigns herself. "Go home, Aurora, and tell our parents that I will come back tomorrow."

Tomorrow? Really? Like a mouse caught in a snare, poor Genovieva has just fallen into a trap. Now she finds out that the certificate can only be given after fifteen days in this establishment. So she must have patience.

But after that... there is no question of getting out.

One day the director of the hospital takes her into a little room. There is a table, a typewriter, a lamp and some books.

"Sit down," says the director. "Here are some books to translate from English into Romanian."

Genovieva had been ready to do anything, as long as she had work. Now she does have a job. With no salary, of course, and imprisoned in this establishment. Oh, how sad it is!

She works in a little office under the constant surveillance of a guard who keeps telling her, "Give up your faith. Stop being a Christian. Then everything will be all right..."

One month goes by... then two, then three. How long will this unjust imprisonment last? Is there nothing that can be done to get her out of there?

The Young Caretaker

"One more page translated!" exclaims Genovieva with a sigh.

"Tired already?" asks the guard who is watching her constantly.

"Oh, no! It's not evening yet!" replies the girl, slipping a new sheet into the old typewriter.

In the light of a poor lamp, she works at a table all day long. She was given a dictionary and a book in English. She has to translate it and type it in Romanian for the director of the institution.

Once again, the girl is bent over the text. But she isn't concentrating. Her thoughts are elsewhere.

It's four months since I've been here, without any news from my family. And it's December. How nice it would be to spend Christmas at home! They are probably not allowed to visit me, nor even to write to me. But I'm sure they haven't forgotten me. Neither has the Lord. He promised to be faithful.

While Genovieva is thinking about this, suddenly a text from the Bible comes to her mind: "I am poor and needy, but the Lord thinks of me." What a blessing this last verse of Psalm 40 is for her!

I don't know how God takes care of me, she repeats to herself, *but I know He does.*

She is right. Already there are Christians in a Western country who know about her situation. They know that she is being kept prisoner for no reason in this hospital. That has to become known, and protests have to be made.

One morning, without the slightest explanation, Genovieva is told that she can go home. Of course, there is no question now of getting that certificate she had come for. But what does it matter? She is free. Christmas at home… what a lovely present!

After all these adventures, Genovieva finds herself in the same condition as before—without work in a country which punishes such people.

"Wouldn't you have a job for me to do?" she asks the elders of her church.

They consult together, then come back to her with a proposal:

"Would you agree to be in charge of cleaning the church?"

"Of course, I would be glad to."

"Then we will take you on. We will give you a signed paper. It will be your 'work contract.' You will work four hours a day. You will open and close the doors. And you will welcome the people."

Would she find it humiliating to change from university student to caretaker? Not Genovieva, who is so happy now. When she takes the broom, she can't help thinking of little Samuel. Didn't Eli give him a similar task in the temple?

So Genovieva walks to the church every day. It is a distance of three miles each way. But at last she has a job.

However, a new problem quickly arises. Even if the work contract protects Genovieva when she is at the church, it has no value if she is checked by the police on the street. Should she consider living in the church?

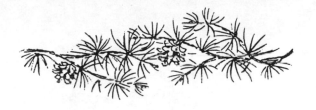

No, that wouldn't be possible. There is no bed and no bathroom there. Could she have them put in? No way! If the police were to discover evidence that someone was living there, they could have the church closed. The risk is too great. But then, what can she do?

Well, I will sleep on a bench, she decides. She knows how to be content with little.

Her new "bed" seems very hard the first nights. Just try sleeping on a hard floor!

And this "bedroom" is rather big for a girl on her own. But she will have to get used to it.

Which one of us would sleep on a bench for a week, a month, or a year? Genovieva will stay there seven years of her life. What will she do when it is very cold at night? Then Genovieva will tremble. She will only have the table cloth as a blanket. Isn't there anyone among her friends who could at least lend her a quilt? Of course, some would be glad to. But if the police ever search this place of worship, they must not find any indication that someone is living there. Otherwise…

It is a winter evening, and for a long time the town has been dark.

We are at a place of worship. The door is locked. So what is going on there at this late hour?

Absolutely nothing, one would think.

Really? Let's go in and have a look…

On the floor, hidden behind the pulpit, a candle is burning. The only source of light and a little warmth, it silently illumines the pages of a Bible. Genovieva is listening to God. Let's not disturb her.

After a while she will blow out the candle. Then, in the cold and dark, Genovieva will have a long talk with her God.

It is in this secret place that a strong missionary vision is to be formed, for a life more and more useful for God.

A Very Useful Child

All of a sudden, without making a noise, the door opens and a little boy appears.

"Hello, Genovieva," he shouts.

Quickly, the girl turns round.

"Oh, Ghiocel! You almost frightened me. How are you?"

"I'm fine. But what are you doing up there?" asks the child, surprised to see his friend on a step ladder beside the window.

"Look, I am cleaning the windows. Tomorrow is Sunday. I'll be glad to see your parents again and mine too, and all the other believers who will come here. Everything must be nice and clean... And

you, Ghiocel, did you happen to be passing by?"

"Yes, and I thought I would stop and say hello to you, Genovieva."

"That's very nice of you, Ghiocel."

"Do you need some help?"

"Oh, yes… you could get me some wood from the yard, and replenish the pile by the stove. And then, do you think you could put some logs on the fire?"

"Of course! It's cold in here."

"I know, I know, Ghiocel! But the church is bigger than an apartment. It is difficult to heat, especially when it's freezing outside as it is these days."

"But… do you really have to live here?"

"Oh, Ghiocel! They made all sorts of trouble for me because I am a Christian. Right now I have this opportunity to work here as the caretaker. But it is better for me to be seen in the street as little as possible. That's why I gave up walking to and from home."

The child remains thoughtful. Something is bothering him. Suddenly he asks another question:

"Where do you wash, Genovieva?"

"At the tap in the yard, just behind here. Next to the little hut for the toilet. Have you never seen it?"

"Of course I've seen it, but… don't you have any hot water?"

"No, not here! But I'm all right. To wash my hair, cold water isn't ideal, but afterwards I dry it next to the furnace. I have to manage the best I can."

"I'll go and get your wood," is all the young boy can say.

Genovieva continues cleaning the windows. After that she will wash the floor, then straighten the benches.

"There! I got all I could," shouts the child when he returns, his arms full of logs. "Shall I make a little pile behind the stove?"

"Yes, please."

"Would it help you if I go and buy you something from the shops like the other day?" asks Ghiocel again a little later.

"Oh, if you have time, I would be very pleased. Here, take some money…"

"And what shall I buy for you?"

"A loaf of bread, some apples, and two or three carrots if you happen to find any."

"Where are you going to cook the carrots?"

"You really want to know everything!" replies Genovieva with a laugh. "I can't cook anything here… But I'll eat them raw. They are very good, even when it's cold. It is a good thing that my brother comes to see me quite regularly. Sometimes he

brings me some food from home. What a blessing that is!

"Be quick, Ghiocel," adds the girl, "and above all be careful!"

"Don't be afraid! I've learned to be careful. See you again soon, Genovieva!"

One hour later Ghiocel is back, proud of what he has bought. Before pushing open the church door, he looks discreetly to the right, then to the left.

No one has followed me, and no one is watching me. I can go ahead.

And he quickly goes in.

"Here's the bread, and here are some carrots," he shouts, very pleased with himself. "You know, Genovieva, no one saw me come here. For the bread, I had to wait in line, but not for too long."

"Thank you, Ghiocel," says the girl, kissing the child on a cold cheek. "You spared me from having to show myself in the street. It's better like that. But how did you find those carrots?"

"I went to three shops. In the third they had some. So I didn't need to look any further. Say, Genovieva," adds the child as

if asking a great favor… "can you tell me a new story from the Bible?"

"Very well. Let's sit down there."

"Not the one about Joseph, nor the one about Peter. I know them already."

"Good! Well… it will be the first chapter of the wonderful story of a little boy like you. When he was your age, his parents taught him to live in the fear of God. It was a good thing that they did, because a little later enemy soldiers arrived in his country. This young boy was taken captive with his friends, all nice boys educated the same way as he was. He was then taken far away to be a servant at the court of a great king who didn't know God. Do you know who this little boy was? His name was Daniel. A whole book of the Bible tells of his adventures. One day…"

Genovieva goes on telling the story as if she were talking to a whole Sunday school class. She only has one listener, but he is so captivated that he could listen for hours.

"Your parents will become worried, Ghiocel," the girl concludes. "Go home quickly now. When you come again, I will tell you the rest of the story."

"All right, Genovieva. I'll come by to-morrow for sure. Will you be here?"

"Oh, yes, Ghiocel, you can be certain of that."

Songs of Joy

"Genovieva! Are you there?"

Because of the dreaded *Securitate*, she still has to hide in her church. She doesn't see anyone enter, as she is cleaning the bottom of a cupboard. But she recognizes that clear voice immediately. It is her friend, Silvia, the pastor's wife.

"Silvia! Oh, how nice of you to come and see me!"

"Here, I've brought you some apples. And then... I have to ask you to do a little job."

"What can I do for you?"

"Well... in a few weeks it will be Christmas. We would like to organize a little celebration here. So, with my husband I was thinking... Would you be able to prepare one or two songs with the children who come with their parents? Everyone would be delighted to hear their sweet little voices."

"What a good idea!" replies Genovieva at once, enthusiastically. "I'll think about it. I'll have to see what songs I can find. As soon as I have something, I'll get the children together."

But very quickly Genovieva is going to make a sad discovery. There are no beautiful Christmas carols and songs for children. Why is it that the Romanian people, who love singing, don't have any songs for children? "Who *used* to love singing," one should say. For years the authorities have done all they can to suppress joy. And the Christians are their first target. It is forbidden for them to compose Christian music. Anyone who does could get fifteen years in prison.

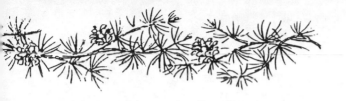

Typing or even photocopying the words of a song is also very risky. Despite the threats, some hymns have been composed. But they are hardly suitable for children. There is such a lack of joy in them. Why is that? Because of where they were composed—in prisons!

I am willing to teach the children some Christmas carols, sighs Genovieva, *but I don't have any. What can I do? Please help me, Lord! Give me a good idea.*

Soon the answer comes, in a very unexpected way. While thinking of her family, Genovieva suddenly remembers a Christian from abroad who visited her parents a few months before.

He left us a cassette of English Christian songs. I must ask my brother to bring it to me, and especially not to forget my cassette player.

What a joy for Genovieva to listen to those songs again! The recording is not very good, but the tunes are so beautiful!

And what if I were to put Romanian words to them—words for Christmas?

A few days later the first song is ready, soon followed by two more.

"Finished! Thank You, Lord!" shouts Genovieva, full of joy. "The children can come."

A few weeks later all the songs from the English cassette have become Christmas carols for the Romanian children.

What a joy for Genovieva's ten little friends!

"Now we know this one well, can you teach us another one? And when can we sing the first one again?" they ask.

Already she has to face a new problem. The children are happy and want more and more songs, but Genovieva doesn't have any more cassettes. What is she to do?

The Sion Choir

"Thank you, Genovieva! Those songs were wonderful!"

"What a beautiful Christmas!"

"The children sang so well… and everything by heart!"

"We had never heard those beautiful songs before."

"The words are so simple!"

"In any case, you should continue, Genovieva."

Those were some of the comments she heard after the holiday. The children had kept their secret well. Their songs were therefore a big surprise for everyone present.

"You should continue…"

Genovieva doesn't forget that. She too thinks that it would be a pity to stop there. She would very much like to continue, but the most important thing is lacking. What is that? Can't she count on those children any more? It's not that. They have the same enthusiasm.

"So… what is missing, Genovieva?"

"Quite simply, more songs. I used all the tunes

on my cassette of English songs… and they became Christmas carols.

"The children already know all of them," sighs Genovieva. "And I don't have another cassette… For weeks I have been trying to find a solution. And the children's desire to sing makes me pray to the Lord for help. Oh! I'll be delighted when His answer comes…"

It is evening, and Genovieva is in the church, which is still her place of refuge. She can't wait to take up her "work" again. While having her frugal meal of two apples and a slice of bread, she looks at the clock several times. On the table are a little radio and the cassette recorder. Patiently Genovieva turns the knob on her radio… Here is some news in Greek. And there is some advertising in German. Here… the reception is disturbed. There, a kitchen recipe is given in French…

"But, Genovieva, you only understand Romanian and English. So why have you been trying for hours to get foreign stations?"

Genovieva has her secret. Maybe she will just happen to tune into a Christian broadcast like the other evening. It doesn't matter whether it is in Italian, Spanish or German—as long as there is at least one song. Then quickly she will press the record button of her cassette player. Afterwards she will have all the time to listen again, then learn the tune in order to write some words in Romanian. Of course, she should begin by asking permission to use this pretty tune. But whom could she ask? She only understands one thing: this song is a Christian song!

"Come, little friends!" Genovieva calls at last. "We have a lot of new songs!"

That's all the children are waiting for. Joyfully they meet with Genovieva one Sunday afternoon, then again the following week. Quietly in this way, a children's choir is formed. It would need a name. Genovieva thinks of the Psalms of David…

"We'll be called the Sion Choir," she decides immediately. "You can join it if you are between six and sixteen. But above all you must have opened your heart to God, and have the courage to tell someone that you are a Christian. You must also promise, in agreement with your parents, to reserve Sundays for the Lord."

If you were there, you who read this story, would you be able to join the Sion Choir?

From that time, on Sunday mornings, during the main service, the children meet in an old wood-shed behind the church. With Genovieva, they study the Bible and learn to pray.

39

But what happens after a few months?

The number of children increases, and the space is limited. So they must come in rotation: twenty one Sunday morning, another twenty the following Sunday.

In the afternoons, everyone meets in the church to learn or practice the songs. And in the evening services, they sing for the church. Teodor, Genovieva's brother, plays the harmonium. Silvia and Nelu accompany them on guitars. The children are happy. They sing everything by heart. Sometimes, between two songs, one of them recites a psalm or says a poem.

Secretly Genovieva continues to pick up Christian broadcasts, to make the words and to teach the songs.

"Be very careful," people tell her sometimes. "If the terrible *Securitate* agents knew what you do, you would be thrown in prison for at least twenty years!"

"I know, I know. But I *am* very careful. I never forget to hide my equipment carefully, and especially the word sheets."

The months go by. All the children are growing up, and each one remains faithful.

Each Sunday evening now the church is filled to capacity. Soon there is no more room. Doors and windows are left open for those who have to stand outside.

Even the people from the neighboring houses have grown into the habit of opening their windows on Sunday evenings.

Now the repertoire numbers 150 songs. The tunes have come from England, France, Italy, Israel, America, Australia, and even from New Zealand. What a variety! But all these songs have this in common: all are about God, and all are sung with joy in Romanian.

The Christians of the town, and even those further away, begin to talk about the Sion Choir.

Then one day Genovieva receives a letter: "Our church would like to hear these children too. We invite you all, if you can come. We are not rich, but we will cover your traveling expenses. Please come and visit us!"

Isn't it dangerous even to consider a trip with all those children? And if Genovieva goes with them, isn't she taking great risks herself? Yes, all that is true. But they are setting out in the Lord's name. He can protect them. This is how the Sion Choir begins to travel, trying however not to attract too much attention.

A Child Disappears

These are hard times for the whole country. Many go hungry. There is mistrust everywhere. People don't talk any more. There are so many sad faces. But when Christians can get together, what joy there is!

The church is still Genovieva's refuge, but she continues to be careful, especially when she has to venture into the street. She then begins by half-opening the door and taking a quick look outside. On the right, no one seems to be watching. On the left, no suspicious car... She can go out.

Today is Monday. There is no time for a walk in the fresh air. Last evening the children's choir sang. The hall was full, in spite of the rain. People came from everywhere, even from the country; their dirty shoes left a lot of mud under the benches. Everything has to be cleaned, and Genovieva does it gladly.

Suddenly, there is a knock and the door opens.

41

A family surrounded by bags and suitcases stands on the doorstep. It is the young pastor who is moving to Iaşi.

"Hello, Genovieva," he says with a big smile. "We finally made it. Now we must look for a place to live. But it will be easier without our luggage. We'll leave it here. By the way, may we leave our son, Aurel, with you for a few hours? He is only eight. There's no need for him to come with us all over the place."

"Of course," replies Genovieva, putting her hand on the child's shoulder. "Come, Aurel, we'll get on fine together, you'll see."

So Aurel stays with Genovieva. They quickly become great friends. Oh, if only things could go as quickly in the search for the apartment! But for several days running, Aurel has to wait at the church with Genovieva.

One evening the young pastor says, "Tomorrow we will have some more things to do. May we leave Aurel with you once again?"

Genovieva seems a bit hesitant.

"I—I'd be glad to take him with me, but it wouldn't be wise. I have to visit Magdalena. She is a Christian lady who shared the Bible with some neighbors. And then because of that she was suddenly put into a psychiatric hospital. She's been there for two weeks. She must feel very lonely."

"Go ahead then, Genovieva! Your visit will do her good. And as for Aurel, we'll leave him at the church. He can wait for you there with a picture book... All right, Aurel?"

42

"All right," says the child.

"I will leave early, and get back as soon as I can," adds Genovieva.

The next day Genovieva goes to the hospital. She is very careful. How many sad memories those long corridors bring back for her! But she is so glad to see Magdalena again!

"What I find the hardest," Magdalena whispers, "is that I couldn't take my Bible with me when they arrested me. I know some verses by heart, and I keep repeating them. But I would like so much to read my Bible, even in secret."

Genovieva makes sure that no one can hear her. Then, in a whisper, she tells her a secret:

"Listen, Magdalena! I managed to hide my Bible in this bag when I came in. I thought we might read a Psalm together in a secret corner. I want to give you this Bible. It will encourage you."

It is all Magdalena can do to keep back her tears.

"I'll come again as soon as I can," adds Genovieva, kissing her friend good-bye. "May the Lord keep you! I must go now, because little Aurel must be waiting for me."

"Well, Aurel, I hope you didn't get too bored," Genovieva asks when she gets back.

"I'm all right," replies the

child, "but I am glad you're back. You know why? I'm hungry. Can you give me something to eat?"

Oh! Genovieva was not expecting that. She doesn't have anything left. She finished the last apple that morning.

"Listen, Aurel! I'll have to go and buy some bread. But you'll have to wait for me again."

"Oh, no! I'm very hungry!"

There is a long line in front of the bakery. Everyone has to have patience, even Aurel…

"I'm back at last," shouts Genovieva cheerfully, opening the door. "Look, what a nice fresh loaf of bread I have. But where are you, Aurel?"

There is no reply.

"Aurel! Ah! Are you playing hide-and-seek? Come, we're going to eat!"

But the child doesn't come.

"Wait, I'm going to find you. You're hiding under a bench… No! Then behind the curtain… You're not there either… Aurel! Stop playing! Come out quickly!"

But no one moves.

Where has he gone? Genovieva wonders, worried. *He was entrusted to me. I am responsible for him. Perhaps he wanted to come to meet me and got lost. Or maybe he is crying somewhere in a corner. It's getting dark. What if someone finds him, and calls the police… No, never! Lord! Please, tell me where he is!*

Genovieva is already outside. She runs back to the bakery. The line is still there, but no Aurel.

She is now in the next road… but she cannot see him. She retraces her steps and passes the church, but he is not there either. Twice, three times, Genovieva goes around the block. It is already half-past eight, and still no sign of Aurel. Suddenly, Genovieva has a strange feeling that she must quickly return to the church… Yes, that's what she is going to do. She hurries back, stops outside, pushes open the gate and… shakes with fear!

Three men are standing there, right in front of her!

The *Securitate* is all she can think of, while in her heart she begs the Lord for help.

The answer comes instantly:

"Hello! Are you Genovieva?" she hears in English. "I am Stephen, and these are my friends."

It doesn't sound like the police. And this nice young man doesn't look like a member of the *Securitate*.

What a joy when Genovieva hears their story!

"Listen! We are Christians. We come from abroad. We are only visiting your town. Someone gave us the address of this church. And guess what we've got with us? Forty Bibles! Where can we leave them?"

"Forty Bibles!" repeats Genovieva, thinking of the one she gave Magdalena.

God didn't allow her to be deprived of His precious Word. Oh, how wonderful He is! But what about little Aurel…? Quickly Genovieva shares her worry with these friends.

"Wait a minute!" one of them says. "I saw a note stuck to the door. Perhaps it's a message for you."

They have a look. And this is what they read: "Dear Genovieva, I came by to pick up my son. He told me that you had gone to buy bread. So I leave you this note, and thank you very much!"

What a relief for Genovieva!

Well-Hidden Treasures

It is one o'clock in the morning at the church. In the darkness, Genovieva turns restlessly on the bench which is her bed. The board is hard. She can feel the freshness of the night. And she doesn't have any blanket. But Genovieva has accepted this lack of comfort for several months, in order to be better hidden. Besides, tonight, it is not that which is preventing her from sleeping. Many thoughts are going through her mind. Last night… the unexpected visit of those three Christians from abroad… the precious contents of their bag. They didn't know where to spend the night. Genovieva gave them her parents' address. That's where they went. One of them is called Stephen. We will meet him again in this long, true story.

So they went on their way. But in the church forty Bibles remained. What a joy, and what a worry too, for Genovieva!

What if the men from the Securitate come and discover this bag? she thinks for a long time. *Tomorrow I will hide all those Bibles. Where shall I put them until I can distribute them?*

But at once Genovieva thinks of friends who would go without food only to have a Bible. Then her heart is filled with joy. So how can she sleep?

Oh, how happy they will be! As long as they can keep the secret to themselves, and not talk too much. Where am I going to hide all these precious Bibles? Well, I have an idea... But I'll need wrapping paper and plastic bags. It's Tuesday. It's a good thing it's not the weekend yet, or too many people would know my secret. I have a few days left... Time to make everything disappear before Sunday morning. No bag of Bibles, no questions asked, and no explanation to give!

The next day Teodor comes to see his sister.

"What have you got in that big bag?" he asks in surprise.

"It is something I need your help with. And it's quite urgent. Listen, Teodor! Last night they brought us forty Bibles. We can't leave them there. They must be distributed as soon as possible. First of all, help me hide this bag. And then... Bring me all the paper and plastic you can find. It doesn't need to be the best quality. I'll explain later…"

"All right. I'll try to get that for you. Hopefully, I'll be back in an hour."

"Here's the first lot," says Teodor, when he returns with a box full of paper. "And I can give

you a hand with it if you like."

"That's nice of you, Teodor, but I will make these parcels at night. It's wiser. Try to find more paper, though. That would be the best help. As for me, I shall be busy this evening. Oh, what a joy!"

It is very late already. But, behind the pulpit, in the feeble light of a candle, Genovieva is at work, crouched on the floor. With a pair of scissors in her hand, she is cutting pieces of paper the right size. Then she will make her parcels.

At two o'clock she is still there… But the big bag of Bibles has become forty little parcels. Yes, forty, because Genovieva has even forgotten her own need. She gave her own Bible to her friend in the psychiatric hospital.

It is getting light now. Genovieva hasn't had much sleep this night.

Will she be able to rest at all? Not yet. She is inspecting all the spots which can serve as hiding places. On a sheet of paper she makes a note of where they are.

She goes outside into the little yard behind the church. Three new hiding places are found and three lines are added to the paper.

What comings and goings! But the list grows longer: On top of the cupboard—in the old dustbin—behind the third board in the fence—under the leaves between the two bushes—at the foot of the old apple tree…

Now the distribution can begin at last. Very carefully, Genovieva puts each parcel in its hiding place. Here, she moves an old piece of furniture. There, she covers with paper the parcel hidden at the bottom of the dustbin. And on it goes…

It is Sunday morning. The Christians arrive at the church. As usual, Genovieva welcomes them. But today she has a special job to do.

"Good morning, Raluca. How are you?" she says, taking her friend's hand.

Then, in a whisper, she adds:

"Listen carefully! There is a parcel for you at the foot of the old apple tree. Take it when no one is looking. Don't open it before you get home…"

"Oh, Lucius and Daniela! Come! I have to speak quietly. Before you go home, take what I prepared for you at the bottom of the dustbin. But be careful!"

Then Genovieva is delighted to see them going very innocently to the designated place and returning with a little plastic bag in their hand.

Later, she learns how excited her friends were to discover a Bible in the parcel they received. Now Genovieva understands why God has allowed her to live in the church. She has a secret mission there. Without any hesitation, she sends word to her friends abroad that she is ready to receive and hide more Bibles.

Then, once a month, at night, a vehicle full of Bibles stops near the church. And when it leaves, it is always empty!

Genovieva does not "give" these Bibles away. It would be too dangerous. All she does is tell people quietly where each parcel is hidden.

And this simple little secret will gently open the way for the Bible to enter hundreds, and even thousands of Romanian homes.

The Little Gypsy Boy

It is Sunday afternoon at the church in Iași. As usual, the children of the Sion Choir have come together. They are all there, from six to sixteen years of age, attentive and full of zeal. Genovieva is such a good leader! At this moment, they are rehearsing one of their favorite songs. What beautiful voices, and what enthusiasm!

Suddenly, almost everyone's eyes turn from Genovieva to the door. What's happening? Genovieva turns round... The song stops in the middle of the refrain.

There he is... shocked by the silence and by everyone staring at him. Who is it? A nine-year-old boy. He was just passing by. He heard singing. Curious, he pushed the door open and risked taking a look inside. Then... fascinated by those voices, he went in.

Oh, how neglected he is! Look at that bushy hair, that worn-out overcoat around his shoulders, and those boots too big for him!

47

"Hello," says Genovieva pleasantly. "Have you come for a visit? Sit down and join us. What is your name?"

"Iulian," replies the child, as if he had made a mistake.

He is a little gypsy boy from the neighboring district.

"Since you have come to see us," continues Genovieva, "we are going to sing especially for you. Would you like that? Are you ready, choir?"

"Yes, yes!" exclaim all the members of the choir.

What a surprise for Iulian! Usually people despise him, a gypsy child. He can't read or write. He doesn't go to school.

But here, he thinks, *they didn't chase me away. They must love me… I'll come back.*

Two days later he does come back. But he is in for a surprise.

"Where are your children?" he asks Genovieva, who is by herself this time.

"They come on Sundays. This is a church."

The child doesn't seem to understand too well. But it doesn't matter.

As time goes by, Iulian becomes a precious little companion for Genovieva. Together, they clean the church, water the flowers, and go and cut the grass in the orchard behind the building. How wonderful that with Genovieva's help he learns to read and write!

48

"Look, Iulian," she says one day, showing the child a nice new copy of the New Testament. "A little more progress, and it will be yours," promises Genovieva.

"Mine?" asks the child in amazement.

"Yes, yes, you'll be able to take it home."

What an encouragement for the little gypsy boy!

Sometimes Iulian comes to the meetings at the church. He always sits in the front row.

"Is there anyone here today who would like to receive Jesus as his Savior?" asks the pastor one Sunday.

Iulian is the first to respond. It is a serious matter for him. Now he too can join the choir. How happy that makes him! What's more, he can even read now. His parents are very proud of him. And Genovieva doesn't forget her promise. What a joy for the child when he goes home with the precious book in his pocket!

From the window, between two walls, Genovieva can see the gypsy quarter. She can even see

the little yard from where the smoke rises. That's where Iulian lives. They cook outside in the open air. Some of them live in huts, others have caravans.

One day while waiting for their parents, some children from the church go for a walk. They reach the gypsy quarter. What do they see all of a sudden? Some men and women sitting outside near a fire which is going out. They seem to be listening. In the midst of them a child is holding a book. He is reading it out loud. That book is the Word of God. And that child is Iulian. He often does that.

Oh, no! An agent from the *Securitate* is watching the district. He notices what is taking place. A few days later the authorities let it be known to the elders of the church that they must no longer receive Iulian.

The police also go to his parents' place and confiscate the New Testament.

"Be careful," they tell those gypsies. "The *credincioşi* (believers) are very dangerous people, often involved in kidnappings or horrible murders. You must no longer let your son go with them. Besides, from now on, we forbid him from leaving the gypsy quarter. If he does, we will put him in prison."

What should they do? As discreetly as possible, the gypsies continue to receive visits from Christians. Genovieva herself takes risks going out to visit Iulian's parents. Oh, what a surprise and what joy that gives Iulian!

But the threats become more serious. Sadly, all contact with Iulian must be broken off.

Nothing happens for many months. There is no more news of Iulian. But the members of the choir continue to pray for their friend. Even though he is alone, Iulian stands firm.

One Sunday afternoon, like the first time, the church door gently opens. It is Iulian. He is so happy to have escaped for a moment, and has come to give his friends a hug.

Edica and Carmen

"What are you doing tomorrow?" Carmen asks her friend Smaranda, on their way back from school.

Carmen is twelve. She is a nice girl, with a thin face and black curly hair.

Smaranda's heart starts beating fast. *Shall I say, "I don't know, read perhaps," to avoid having problems?* But Smaranda doesn't want to lie. She knows very well what she will do, but giving any details is very risky. If she says plainly that she is an active member of the Sion children's choir, Carmen may talk about it. At school the teacher will know. Then, Smaranda will be humiliated in front of everyone, perhaps even beaten.

"Listen, Carmen," she says resolutely. "I belong to a children's choir. Tomorrow afternoon we will have a rehearsal. Would you like to come and listen to us sing?"

The next day Carmen is at the church. Her eyes are wide open, and she listens attentively.

"It's beautiful!" she tells Smaranda. "But... I don't understand. These songs talk about God and Jesus... what does that mean?"

Up to now Carmen has never heard these names. At twelve years of age she knows nothing about God, and nothing about Jesus either. Her parents are atheists. They don't believe in anything. How could they have told her about her Creator?

"Do you think I can come back and listen another time?" asks Carmen.

"Of course," replies Smaranda, very happy. "If your parents agree."

So Carmen comes back to the church. She also brings Edica, her younger sister of ten.

"We're going to meet my friend Smaranda," she tells her parents.

The sisters take part in two, then three rehearsals. Soon they know a song almost by heart.

"I would love to belong to the choir," Carmen tells her friend. "What do I have to do to join?"

"Listen, Carmen, when I wanted to become a member of the choir, I was asked if I knew Jesus, and if I had opened my heart to Him. I had taken that step. It's the first condition for being accepted in the choir."

"I would like Jesus to be my Savior too," says Carmen timidly. "But... what do I have to do?"

"At the next choir practice, ask Genovieva. She will explain it to you."

At the following choir rehearsal a nice girl talks to Carmen and her sister Edica.

"It's been a good practice," says Genovieva, "and now we are going to pray for the evening program. Let's ask God to help us, and to encourage many people by these songs."

These children learn not only to sing, but also to talk with God. They certainly need Him, as they are often mocked at school.

So they pray very simply, out loud, one after another. And suddenly, this is what they hear:

"Lord Jesus, I would like to receive You right now. Come and live in my heart. I, Carmen, give my heart to You."

"I, Edica, too."

The children continue praying, but now they ask God to bless these two friends. That moment of prayer concludes with the verse of a song. Then, spontaneously, a child shouts:

"Welcome to the family of God, Carmen and Edica!"

And, full of joy, all the young singers begin to clap.

But one day their parents discover that the two little girls are meeting Smaranda at church.

"We must stop that," they decide. "If they want to believe in God, that's all right with us. But

this is going too far. We will have trouble."

"Dad... Mom... please let us go!" beg the two girls. "It does us so much good!"

Their parents do recognize that Edica and Carmen are happier. But they still don't want to hear about it.

On Sunday mornings the two girls leave very quietly, while their parents are still sleeping. Their parents are tired, because work begins before six o'clock every morning.

When they get back from church, there is always a storm. The two girls are scolded, their hair is pulled, they are hit, they are threatened.

"And don't you let us find you praying in your bedroom any more!"

But despite all that, Carmen and her sister persevere. They don't want to cause trouble for their parents, but they are so happy with Jesus in their hearts. They want to continue going to church. Too bad if they are beaten!

"We are getting nowhere," their parents admit. "Let's use school..."

To go to school, like all pupils, Carmen and Edica have to wear their uniform. On their sleeve is the number of their school. For them it is the number 4. And each of them has her own number: 800 for Carmen, 931 for Edica.

"Let's take all their other clothes away," their parents decide. "They won't dare to go to church in their uniforms. It's too easy to be seen and reported..."

The following Sunday Genovieva sees the two girls coming in their school uniforms.

On their way out they are noticed, and reported to the police.

The next day at school, Carmen and Edica are severely punished. They have to stay at the very back of the class. And their friends are forbidden to speak to them.

Will they give up at last? No.

For five years Carmen and Edica will not miss a single Sunday at church.

"I wonder if they are hiding Christian books in their bedroom," their parents say to one another. "We must take them away!"

Carmen and her sister have indeed received a book. It has some beautiful stories from the Bible, and pretty colored pictures. This book is their treasure. It is the only one they have. One Sunday morning, before leaving, they decide to hide it under their mattress. Then they pray that their parents don't find it.

God will answer their prayer, but not in the way they think.

I am going to search everywhere, their mother says to herself. *If they are hiding something, I must find it. Let's have a look under the mattress. Aha! I knew it! Whatever is this book?* Nervously, she begins turning the pages. Then she stops at a beautiful picture of a flock of sheep and a shepherd. She begins to read... and suddenly to cry! Then, without a word, she puts on her coat, leaves the apartment, and goes straight to the church.

This Sunday morning, for the first time, she hears the Gospel. Touched, she too opens her heart to the Savior of the world. Everything is going to change. This mother has become a Christian. The perseverance of the two little girls has borne fruit.

Maria's Clothes

It is Sunday morning, and the believers have sung their closing hymn. Suddenly someone seizes Genovieva's arm. It is Maria. She wants to talk with her in private.

"Listen, Genovieva," she is soon telling her friend. "I too am watched by the secret police. I no longer feel safe... Could I sleep here, like you?"

"Of course, if the elders of the church agree. But... you will have to be very careful, you know."

Before giving more explanation, Genovieva makes sure that no one can overhear this conversation.

"Nobody should know that you are living here. And are you ready to sleep without a mattress, without a blanket, and without a pillow?"

"Why? I'll bring everything I need!"

"No, Maria, you can't! If we get searched, the *Securitate* would

have proof that someone lives here. Then…"

"Then what?" asks Maria naively.

"They could even close the church. You understand?"

Maria nods.

"Listen," continues Genovieva. "For months my only blanket has been the tablecloth. And sometimes it is very cold. The church isn't easy to heat. But if you are content with a bench for a bed, you can come."

Maria does not hesitate: "I don't care for comfort, as long as I don't have other troubles."

She now shares the refuge with Genovieva. She will spend about a year there.

Poor Maria suffers from rheumatism, and the cold is her great enemy. She has to fight it. But what can she do in winter, in a church which is so difficult to heat? Maria has found an unusual solution. She wears all the clothes she possesses. Five dresses, several jackets, three scarves and two bonnets. She looks quite impressive!

54

She is quite a character, this Maria! But this afternoon her variety of clothes is going to be very useful.

"Wait for me," Genovieva tells her 'roommate.' "I have to go and buy some food."

Prudently, she first takes a look in the street. Nothing unusual to the right, nothing to the left. So she can go out.

She passes a lady who takes no notice of her. Then two boys in their school uniforms.

As long as the line isn't too long, Genovieva says to herself, as she walks along at a quick pace.

Do you see that old wall, covered with ivy? It is the same height as Genovieva. She is going to pass it. The poor girl doesn't know that a policeman is hiding right behind it. Suddenly Genovieva sees him. But it's too late to turn back.

Did our friend appear a little hesitant? Quite possibly.

"Where are you going?" asks the man from the *Securitate.*

"I need some bread… I'm going to buy some."

"Show me some identification."

"I've just come out of the church, a hundred yards from here," Genovieva tries to explain. "I left my bag there, with my papers."

"Well, go and get them then!"

Genovieva obeys at once. On her way she begs God for help…

She comes to the gate of the church. Before going in, she turns round quickly. The policeman is coming in her direction…

In theory, he hasn't the right to arrest someone in a place of worship. But in front of the church it is very different.

Genovieva hurries into the building.

Maria jumps. But before she has time to ask questions…

"Quick!" says Genovieva, "give me your clothes! Hurry, Maria, please! Your top dress, your jacket, quick!"

Not knowing what to say, Maria takes off one of her dresses.

"What do you want…?"

"Quick, one of your scarves… and give me your stockings!"

Maria obeys like a robot, not understanding anything.

"Your bonnet too!" pleads Genovieva, while Maria throws her jacket to her.

"Quick… there! Thank you very much, I can go! See you!" adds Genovieva, as she goes out of the church.

She looks funny in that dress which is too big for her. Really she looks ridiculous with those pleated stockings on her thin legs, which are trembling a little, to be sure.

Where is she going? wonders Maria, flabbergasted.

Hardly outside, Genovieva feels a shiver go down her spine.

He is there, next to the gate. He looks at her with apparent surprise.

It's not the one I am expecting, the policeman is surely thinking, as an old woman, slightly bent, passes by him.

Poor man… he will be waiting a long time!

The little grandmother, who has been limping, disappears at the corner of the road. Then, all of a sudden, she begins to run like a deer.

Soon she rushes to a door, knocks, and disappears into the house. She is at the home of some Christians. These friends are very surprised to see her in such an attire…

The father has a car. After dark, he will take Genovieva back to her place of refuge. Then, at last, Maria will be able to understand.

"You know," Genovieva admits to her, "I often wanted to laugh at seeing you wear all those clothes. But never have I appreciated your walking wardrobe as much as today!"

Shadows in the Night

The water starts to boil at last on the old electric heater Genovieva uses at the church. Soon she will warm up a little with a cup of tea.

While waiting, she takes from her pocket a letter which she begins to read with interest.

"Another request!" our friend exclaims. "Well, we will have to go…"

"Please," writes the elder of a church in another town, "come with your children's choir, come and sing for us! Your traveling expenses will be reimbursed."

Genovieva is used to receiving such requests. God is using and blessing the Sion Choir. Concerts are organized here and there, and that gives great joy to its members. They travel quite regularly all year round, winter or summer. Sometimes they travel by train. Then they all meet at the train station, very early on Sunday mornings.

But other times they go on foot, by bus, ox-cart, even by boat, to towns and villages all over the country. These sixty young singers are from six to sixteen years old. They are overflowing with joy and people love their singing. How did they learn to sing so well? By persevering. They have never been afraid of long rehearsals, even during the holidays.

Besides learning to sing, they also know how to pray. That is the secret of their success. They all need to be protected. If one of them has problems at school because he is a Christian, they all pray for him. If they have to face threats or persecution, everyone talks to God about it.

The police would love to shut everything down, but it is not easy to arrest so many children at once. It seems much simpler to attack those who bring them together. Genovieva would have reason to be afraid, but she is confident in the One who can keep her.

At this time Maria is not living at the church. Genovieva is there by herself. It is a blessing for her that her parents and one of her brothers come to see her three times a week. It is a precious thing to be able to pray as a family.

This evening, as she lies down on her bench to try to sleep, Genovieva hesitates.

I don't know why, but I don't feel at ease… Perhaps I should sleep somewhere else. But where? Oh, I know…

Under the floor of the platform is a large tank. Sometimes it is filled with water for baptisms. Otherwise, it is empty.

That's where I'll spend the night—in there! Genovieva decides.

She goes down into the tank and quickly replaces the boards above her.

A little after two o'clock in the morning, Genovieva wakes up with a start. Someone is speaking loudly just behind the door of the church. Now… someone is trying a key in the lock!

From her hiding place, Genovieva holds her breath. The door creaks open… Genovieva prays. Heavy steps hammer the floor. There are at least two men. For about five long minutes the beam of their flashlight searches everywhere.

"No one!" a voice concludes. "She isn't here!"

"Let's look a bit further," another voice adds.

Genovieva does not move…

Finally the light goes away, and so do the steps.

Then, very gently, one board of the platform comes up, then another… Out come a head and shoulders, then a whole body.

Exactly what I thought, Genovieva says to herself. *They know how to open doors, but they have not yet learned to close them.*

Don't trouble yourselves, policemen, I'll take care of it!

Courageously she gets up and goes to close the door.

Now I can sleep in peace. They won't come back.

The weeks go by. The Sion Choir continues to travel. Oh, how much the *Securitate* would like to make these children shut up!

"We must get the leader!" they say. "We will watch her parents' house. We will know when she sleeps at home. And if she isn't there, we'll be able to catch her at the church."

But what are they planning?

To arrest her? To imprison her? Even worse—to kill her!

One night a car from the *Securitate* comes to a gentle stop just in front of the church. From there, the chief of the secret police will be able to watch everything that happens.

In the church hall Genovieva is not sleeping. Then what is she doing at midnight, crouched behind some furniture in the dim light of a candle? Perhaps she is reading her Bible. Perhaps she is jotting down the words of a new song.

Suddenly she straightens up anxiously. She has just heard a noise…

There is no doubt: someone is climbing over the fence in front of the church!

Quickly Genovieva puts out the candle.

There, someone is knocking at the door! What shall I do now?

"Open!" she hears. "Open! We know you are there!"

More knocking at the door…

"Open, Genovieva! Open at once, Genovieva! This is a police order!"

Protect me, Lord! What shall I do? Tell me quickly!

With a master key they get the door open. It turns on its hinges. They come in. Soon the beam of their flashlight will sweep one wall after the other…

Where is this girl they are looking for? Silently she hurries to the other end of the hall. Her thoughts are racing in her head:

If at least I could escape behind the church, she thinks. *From that side there is no fence to cross. The ground slopes down, but I know the path very well. How often I hid Bibles there! There is a door here, but it must be blocked. It is never used.*

Genovieva tries to push it—and it opens with no problem. It must have been closed for months, without anyone realizing that it was not locked.

Quickly Genovieva gets out. And the door closes behind her. The bird has flown!

She comes to the old apple tree… then to the low wall which she only has to step over… Further on is the road. Quickly Genovieva runs to some friends…

Oh! how much this verse from the Bible means to her: "The Lord is my helper. I will not be afraid. What can man do to me?" It has been underlined in her Bible for a long time, in chapter 13 of the letter to the Hebrews.

Be strong, Genovieva! There are more trials to come. But the One who keeps you is always watching. Never forget that!

In the Forest
of Wolves

It is December again. In the United States, England and other countries, the shop windows have been full of wonderful gifts for several weeks. But in Romania there is nothing of all that.

Everything that can make you think of Christmas is forbidden. A child has even been severely punished for drawing a Christmas tree!

But this year, for Christmas Day, the Sion Choir has been invited to sing. This large family is expected at the other end of the country, 300 miles from Iași. Several pastors took this risk. And the local Christians are paying the traveling expenses.

Genovieva starts by looking at a map. Then she quickly understands that this "expedition" will not be easy.

"Look, Teodor," she says to her brother, "we'll be able to travel by train to the nearest town. But after that... the village where we are expected is 60 miles from there. And there are no buses at that time."

"Should we ask the local believers to come and pick us up in their cars?"

"I don't think so, Teodor. We did that somewhere else, and it caused us trouble with the police.

Since then, they have forbidden that kind of transport for our choir. A convoy of cars like that would not go unnoticed. But I have an idea. Marta is our friend... You know where she works?"

"In a travel agency, I believe."

"Yes, at the Tourist Office. She is responsible for reserving buses for tourists visiting the country. In theory you must be a member of the Party to have the right to hire a bus. But, who knows? Perhaps Marta could arrange something for us. I must talk with her about it."

"No problem," says Marta. "Sixty children and five adults for December 25. All right. You can count on me. Your bus will be waiting for you at the train station."

So everything is arranged. The children cannot wait. They are very excited. And how hard they work to learn even more songs by heart!

Christmas Day arrives at last. Very early, everyone meets at the station. Oh! how many words of advice are given...

"We entrust you with Mihaela, our youngest little girl. You know her, Genovieva. She is still fragile. But so thrilled to be going!"

"Don't worry, Liliana! I'll take good care of her."

"Ghiocel has just got over tonsillitis. Make sure that he is well wrapped up. Thank you!"

Genovieva reassures all the parents. Yes, she will be very attentive. Yes, she will take care of everyone. Yes, everything will be fine.

The first part of the journey goes as planned. When they arrive at the destination...

"Look," shouts one of the boys, "the bus is already here!"

"Wow... a luxury bus!" Genovieva realizes. "I wonder if it is really ours. We'll see... Yes, it's the one. We are really spoiled!"

The driver starts by counting the children. Then he opens the doors and tells them to get in.

"Off we go," he says, turning the key in the ignition.

They leave the town. Very soon they are in the open country. Then they enter a forest. Are there wolves? Quite possibly. With their eyes glued to the windows, the children gaze outside.

The weather is cold. It begins to snow. Soon it will be dark. At the wheel, the driver seems indifferent to the children's joy. He wonders, though, what this party of kids can be doing in this area. But that's none of his business.

A child begins to hum the last song they learned. Those next to him start to sing too, and the whole group joins in. They love this new refrain.

Suddenly, quite abruptly, the bus stops at the side of the road. The engine shuts off.

Red with anger, the driver turns towards Genovieva:

"You're Christians!"

Genovieva doesn't know what to say. Then the driver stands up, opens the door, and…

"Out!" he shouts. "Everyone get off this bus! Off! I am not taking you another yard!"

All the children stop singing, stunned with shock.

"But…" intervenes Genovieva calmly, "we paid for this trip. Things are in order. We have…"

"Out!" yells the driver.

"Please," insists Genovieva, "I am responsible for these children. It's getting dark. It's cold. You can't leave us here. We don't even know where we are!"

"Everyone off!" repeats the driver, unbending. "I don't transport Christians!"

What can they do? To get off the bus in the middle of the forest, and in the dark—really that is not possible. Once more Genovieva tries to argue with the man:

"I beg you, Sir, don't leave us here! Drive us at least to the next village!"

In the middle of the aisle a child kneels down. His hands are together. And another child does the same. They are praying silently. Soon all the members of the choir have their heads bowed. All their lips are moving, but only God can hear.

The driver turns round. Will they at last decide to obey him? What does he see? His bus full of praying children! He takes out his handkerchief and wipes his forehead. He coughs nervously. He moves his hands in his pockets, then through his hair…

All of a sudden he gets up, shuts the door, and with tears in his eyes, takes his place at the wheel. Then he starts the engine again. Never has the hum of an engine sounded so pleasant to the passengers!

"I'll take you where you want," says the driver, defeated.

"Thank you, thank you very much!" everyone replies.

That evening the driver is there to listen to "the most beautiful Christmas carols sung by the little travelers," as he himself will say. When it is time to go back after that beautiful evening, it is a friend who drives them.

The Police Arrive

"All right," said Mr Coroamă, "we will be happy to have you all in our house. It's plenty big enough, you'll see!"

Mr Coroamă is a very active Christian. He has done everything to organize this four-day visit of the Sion Choir in his village.

We are now in the extreme north of the country, only two miles from the Russian border. Vicovu de Sus is a large mountain village. Autumn adorns it with its most beautiful colors. But it is already cool.

Making the most of the holiday season, several churches from the area have invited the fifty children and their six leaders. This last evening the choir will sing at Vicovu de Sus.

What activity there has been in the Coroamă family for the last three days! The house is full to capacity. There are straw mattresses spread over the floor everywhere, even in the attic. It is a bit overcrowded, but what a joy it is for everyone!

For the meals, long tables have been set up in the garden, behind the house. Christian ladies from the village take turns to come and do the cooking.

For the first three evenings the young singers were welcomed in packed churches. The village children gave them a big bouquet of flowers.

Preparing the program was no small thing. But each of the six adults on the trip has his own job. Rodica makes sure the children are dressed properly. Perhaps the boys have stains on their clothes. Is the girls' hair combed? Vieru cleans their shoes. He also keeps order in this big family. Silvia copies and distributes the evening program. Everything must be well organized. They can't hesitate in public over the order of songs. Elena is responsible for the equipment. Teodor tunes the instruments. And Genovieva? She watches over everything. If the children become too excited, she keeps her smile, raises her hand, and calm returns. And then… there are unexpected situations.

"Genovieva, my shoe-lace is broken. Have you got another one?"

"Genovieva, I've just lost a button. Can you sew it on for me?"

"Genovieva, I've got a toothache. Do you have an aspirin?"

Before each performance, the big family joins together to ask God's help. They go over the most difficult songs again.

This afternoon everyone is in the garden, when an unexpected visitor appears at the gate. It is a plainclothes policeman, with a severe face and a broad-brimmed hat.

Suddenly, all the children are quiet.

The police officer comes into the garden. He looks at the whole group, stares at Genovieva, and points to her with his finger.

"You! Come with me to the police station!"

Everyone knows what that can mean.

"Me? Why?" Genovieva asks.

"Don't ask questions. Come!"

Quickly she puts on her shoes and tidies her hair.

"Pray for me," she whispers to the children, while the policeman waits at the gate, his back turned.

"But… what are you doing?" Genovieva asks three of the smallest children.

Spontaneously they have surrounded her with their arms.

"Don't go!" they tell her.

Four, five… twenty other children come and crowd around her. The circle gets bigger and tighter. Genovieva can no longer take a single step.

"Don't go, please!" repeat the voices of fifty children.

The policeman is getting impatient… The smaller children are beginning to cry.

"Don't go, Genovieva! Don't go!"

Only children dare to oppose an order from a policeman like that!

Genovieva tries in vain to get out.

"Well, are you coming?" shouts the policeman.

But the more the man insists, the more the crying increases, and the more impenetrable the wall of children becomes.

Puzzled by this uproar, some neighbors gather near the fence. That is the last thing the police want. Caught between the curious people in the street and the children's crying, the policeman abruptly leaves.

What a sigh of relief! A little boy thanks God out loud.

But their tears have hardly dried, when the noise of an engine approaches. A car stops near the gate. The same man gets out, followed by an officer in uniform. It is as if he is hiding behind his dark glasses.

Immediately, the circle forms again.

"Miss Genovieva," the officer says very courteously. "We are under orders to take you to the police station for a simple identity check. Please come with us. In half an hour you will be back."

But the children don't trust him.

"Don't go!" they cry again.

The officer gets upset. No longer able to make himself heard, he orders Genovieva to come by making signs to her.

"Little friends, I have to go… So let me pass! Make room for me!"

But it is a waste of effort. The little singers do not move.

"Do you hear?" roars the policeman.

"Come! We are waiting for you!"

"I know, but I can't move," replies Genovieva, pressed on all sides. "I can't move an inch!"

The spectators continue to gather, and the two policemen feel more and more embarrassed. Nervously they exchange a few words, then disappear into their vehicle which starts up immediately.

Once again the children can breathe. But two boys, Cornel and Iulian, decide to set a guard at the gate. Half an hour later they come running into the garden…

"A car is coming!" they shout. "It has three aerials!"

"Three aerials? That is the *Securitate*!"

Quickly the wall of defense rises around Genovieva.

Two other gentlemen get out of the vehicle. So as not to frighten the children, they stay at a distance.

"Miss," they say calmly. "We have received an order. You must come with us."

Genovieva makes a sign that she has understood. She tries to clear a way towards the policemen, but a new wall prevents her. The terrified children form a hedge which no one can cross.

"Don't go! Don't go!" they all shout, crying.

The two policemen are powerless. It is indeed the first time that they have come up against "an army of children." Then, they turn round and never return.

Oh, how this experience draws the members of the choir together! This evening their songs will sound more vibrant than ever. There is something about them which cannot be defined—something of heaven!

A Hiding Place for the Night

"Tell me, Mom… where is Dad? Why does he go somewhere else to sleep all the time?" asks little five-year-old Marius.

Elena gives a long sigh… What can she reply to the child that would be true, without saying too much? The less he knows about it the better.

"Listen, my dear," explains Elena, caressing her child's hair. "You know that your dad teaches the Bible. He is a pastor. The leaders of our country are against God. They don't like Dad's work at all. The police would love to arrest him and put him in prison. If he were here in the evenings or at night, they would easily find him. So… he has to hide."

"Where does he hide, Mom?"

Elena would love to satisfy her child's curiosity. But it would be dangerous. Little Marius could repeat what he is told. And that could mean more problems for his father.

"Where? I can't tell you now, my dear. But I will tell you one day, I promise. All right?"

"All right."

And the little boy slips quietly into bed.

As a friend of the family, Genovieva knows the situation. In the evenings, before lying down on her bench to sleep, she often prays for her pastor. Now and again he stops for a short time at the church. In fact, he has just arrived.

"Look, Genovieva," he says, taking a letter from his pocket...

"I was afraid it would come to that!" exclaims Genovieva after reading it. "Every day, all over the country, they teach children at school that God does not exist. And the children in our choir sing to the glory of God. That really upsets them!"

"The authorities spread false rumors about the believers: 'Beware of those *credincioși*,' they say. 'Those gangsters kidnap children and commit murders. They are dangerous people!' But they are wasting their time. People keep crowding into this place to hear these beautiful songs. So now they are trying other methods. Threats, for example, like this letter."

All the pastors in the country have just received this same letter. What does it say? From now on it is forbidden to invite the Sion Choir to sing in public. It is also forbidden to compose songs, and those who do so are threatened with prison.

"But we must persevere," the pastor hastens to add, "even if some of us will have to face interrogation about the choir."

"And even if drivers' licenses have been confiscated from friends who transported the choir..."

"Do you see, Genovieva? The police cannot easily attack the children. So they are attacking those who invite them to their churches."

"Be on your guard!" says Genovieva.

"Oh, yes! I have to hide for a while. Do you know where I spend the night?"

"Yes, Elena told me the secret. May God keep you! I often ask Him to. And may He protect you from the cold."

Where is this courageous pastor's hiding place? Soon it will be dark. Let's follow him. We'll see at which home he stops. At which home? No, he doesn't stay at another home. Staying with other Christians would be just as dangerous.

Look! He is going out of the

town towards the hill. But there are no houses up there, except for the old monastery.

Is that where he is going? No. But the hill is almost completely wooded. Look...! The man is leaving the path. He walks on, pushing his way through branches and bushes.

Now he can no longer be seen. Did he fall? No, he is lying down and covering himself with a pile of dead leaves. What? Is that where he spends the night? Yes, for a month already, despite the cold.

"Aren't there wolves?" Genovieva asks, concerned for her pastor.

"Wolves? It is a little too close to the town for them. But they wouldn't scare me. They are not as dangerous as the *Securitate*! You know, Genovieva, once I had to hide for three months in the mountains. I used to eat berries. There I did see wolves, but they didn't do me any harm. When they came close, I would speak to them. Once I told them, 'You come to visit me so late! But I'm sleepy! Good night, friends!'

"And let me tell you what happened to me one night," says the servant of God. "I was so tired, and it was very cold. Then I prayed, 'Lord, cover me with a blanket, or I will freeze to death.' I fell asleep, and that night I wasn't cold at all. Do you know why? Listen! It was still dark when I woke up the next morning. I tried to stretch a little. Then, I was amazed to see an animal!

"It got up and ran off. Was it a stray dog? Was it a wolf? I do not know. But it spent the night right next to me. God is so wonderful! He couldn't have sent me a warmer blanket."

A little later—just before Christmas 1975—Marius and Cristina's father suddenly finished his life's journey down here. He was found dead in his car. The police talked about an accident. But there was no sign of it on the road. And there wasn't the slightest scratch on the car! This servant of God was assassinated. By whom? You can guess.

Elena remained faithful to the Lord. Marius and Cristina grew up. Both of them also sang in Genovieva's choir. At a very young age, Marius played the guitar very well. He accompanied the choir. You can see here Elena and her two dear children.

After high school, Cristina studied the guitar at the Conservatory. Her brother Marius went to university. He wanted to become a specialist in Hebrew and Greek. His goal was to work on a new translation of the Bible.

The Surrounded Hill

There is something moving on that old trunk covered in ivy…

"Look… a pretty nuthatch!" exclaims Genovieva, filled with wonder at the beautiful creature.

All her friends have stopped talking to watch the bird. Head down, the nuthatch takes little jumps down the trunk of the tree, looking for the smallest insect to eat.

The grass is green, the trees are in blossom. The countryside is singing on this beautiful April day. It is Easter morning.

In this peaceful clearing, on the top of the hill, about thirty young people are sitting in a circle.

All are committed believers, and they have decided to spend the day apart, far from the noise of the town, far from the worries of college or work. They will be able to read the Bible, pray and sing in perfect freedom. What a joy!

Easter! After being crucified and put in a tomb, Jesus came back to life. Their Savior is alive, yes, really alive! They must rejoice.

When they woke up this morning, the sky was blue. A real Easter Sunday. What a joy for everyone! Mr Ulf, their great friend from Denmark, had told them, "If it is nice weather, I'll come with you." He is an experienced Christian, a man used by God, and whom the police would very much like to keep quiet. Genovieva saw him for the first time when she translated for him, from English into Romanian. She will never forget that evening…

As she was repeating his words sentence after sentence, Genovieva had suddenly felt touched herself. And there, in the secrecy of her heart, she had received Jesus Christ as her Savior. How many things had resulted from that! Expulsion from university, subtle persecution, the need to hide, but also the joy of being a true Christian, experiencing the protection of God, sharing the Gospel with children, starting the Sion Choir…

They set out, each one with his Bible and his picnic lunch in a bag.

To get to the clearing, one can follow the road which spirals around the hill. But there is a much shorter way to get there. It is a path steeper than the road that climbs straight up the hill through the forest. That is the way the young people went.

Their dream has become a reality. Together they can now enjoy the fresh air. They can see part of the town below, through the branches, but they can't hear the noise. It is so peaceful up there.

"Let's sing!" one of them says.

Their voices blend with the buzzing of bees and the songs of birds… What a joy it is to thank the Lord for Easter in complete freedom!

Now Mr Ulf shares some of the wonders of the Bible. In places of worship secret agents can easily infiltrate the believers. But here he can talk openly, with no fear of being spied on… It is a special moment, a wonderful air of freedom!

Hours go by without any disturbance. Now our friends are singing the last song to close this Easter service. What fervor there is in those voices! It is not a lullaby which makes you fall asleep, but a hymn of victory to the glory of God.

But all of a sudden, just before the refrain, they hear the distant sound of an engine. They look at each other with a feeling of insecurity. Everyone thinks the same thing.

"It's a motorized vehicle!"

"…coming up the hill!"

"Listen! Barking of dogs!"

"The secret police are after us, no doubt about it. How did they know that we…"

"Oh! they are well informed, they have eyes and ears everywhere. Even at church when we talk among ourselves, you never know who might be listening!"

From among these young people, Costel, Ioan and Vasile have already been followed by the police. So has Genovieva. They escaped by running fast, with

God's help. But this time, where can they run to? They are on top of a hill, and the *Securitate* vehicles are surrounding them.

"Let's run off down the path!"

"No! the dogs will soon be on our tracks!"

"Then let's all pray!"

Fervent prayers quickly replace their songs. It is not poems they are reciting, but real cries of distress and calls for help… Do these young Romanians remember the story of David? He also found himself in danger on a mountain, surrounded by enemies. His life was threatened. But God intervened and drove them away. What did He do? You can read about it in the Bible (1 Samuel chapter 23, from verse 25).

God hasn't changed. He still does miracles to protect His people. On this beautiful Easter day, these young friends are going to experience one. It is written in their Bible that "nothing is impossible with God." They know that very well. But now they are going to see it with their own eyes.

The cars get nearer… and the barking too. In the clearing the Christians are praying. What will God do to save them? Will He send helicopters? There is no need. All He needs is some thick clouds, and wind to blow them above the hill. Look! In a moment the sun disappears. The sky becomes very dark…

Suddenly there is a powerful flash of lightning, followed by a loud clap of thunder.

Then a powerful storm breaks over the hill. Strong gusts of wind tear the blossoms off the trees. It looks like snowflakes swirling everywhere.

Where are the Christians going to find shelter? There is nowhere to go. But getting wet doesn't matter to them. For them, this big storm is their refuge. Now is the time to escape. They run down the wooded slopes, grasping hold of bushes so as not to slip, hanging on to branches so as not to fall…

In record time, they arrive at the bottom of the hill. They are dripping wet and scratched all over, but they are free!

The secret police have reached the clearing. They too have to face the storm, and have nowhere to shelter.

"Go after them!" they shout to their dogs.

But how can the dogs smell the fugitives in the rain?

Wet and muddy, the believers make a dash for Silvia's parents' house. There they are safe.

"The Lord was with us!" they repeat. "On Easter morning He rose from the dead. He rolled back the stone from the entrance to the tomb. And this same Almighty God sent rain and made the wind blow. What a beautiful Easter Day!"

Edidia's Visit

It is past midnight, but two girls are still talking in a little attic.

"Have you been a believer for long?" asks Genovieva.

Edidia's face lights up in a beautiful smile as she tells her story:

"When I was six, Dad, Mom, my two sisters and I had only a kitchen and one bedroom to live in. It wasn't easy. But my parents were Christians. One day I was alone with Mom. She had had enough of that little place. She told me, 'Edidia, we must pray for somewhere else to live.' And we did so at once. The same week someone asked my parents, 'Are you by any chance looking for a larger apartment? I have one for you.' Soon after that we moved… Since that day I've known that God hears us, and that He answers when His children are in need."

Who is Edidia, this nice girl of eighteen, and what is she doing at Genovieva's? We will soon see.

71

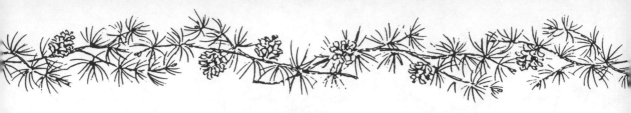

Yesterday, Saturday, Genovieva was at home. It was snowing hard—a time to stay indoors. In the snow the last house on that little road was less noticeable.

The snowflakes were swirling everywhere, and under snow-covered umbrellas, three people—a man, a woman and a girl—came walking along. They seemed to be looking for something.

"This is certainly the house," said one of them. "Let's see the number… Thirty-one. We're there. Wait here! I'll go through the gate and knock at the door."

A girl in her twenties appeared at the door.

"Hello! What do you want?" she said cautiously. *"Pace!"**

This single word put her at ease. In Romanian it means "peace." The believers like it very much. They greet each other with it. *"Pace"* is their identity card, their password, a sort of "I fear God too."

"Do come in!" said the girl at once.

"We are looking for a certain Genovieva…"

"Oh, really? Shhh!… Shut the door! There! I *am* Genovieva!"

"Well, what a joy it is to meet you! My wife and I do what we can to share the Gospel with children. We heard about your children's choir, though we live in a little town in the middle of the country. We were very pleased to hear all about it. So we came by train with our friend here.

* Pronounced *pah-chay*.

And the stranger continued:

"Edidia is studying to become a teacher. She does a good job teaching Sunday school. She wanted very much to meet you, to learn about the way you work with children—if you agree."

When Edidia arrived at Genovieva's place, she felt a little intimidated. Several young people were there, talking to Genovieva's parents and her brothers and sisters. Almost all of them were students. It was a warm atmosphere, but still you could tell that these young people were not there just to have a good time.

"Every Christian takes risks simply because he believes in God," said Genovieva.

She seemed to know what she was talking about. She could understand the problems these young people were having, and she had a way of encouraging each one of them.

After the whole team has had a good meal of corn mush, Genovieva gives all her attention to Edidia:

"If you are happy with that couch in the corner, you can sleep here. Is that all right?"

"I don't have anything better at home. If you could see what I sleep on…"

The two friends settle down for the night in the little attic. The next day will be very busy. There will be no time for conversation. So even though it is already late, Edidia goes on with her story:

"God knew that we were going to need a bigger house. Soon He sent Christians with Bibles to us from Geneva and neighboring France. Delivery was always made in the middle of the night. First someone would come and knock quietly at our door. 'Pace!' they would say, in a low voice. 'We have our car up the street. It's full of Bibles.' When the unloading had to be done quickly, the parcels were first put in our bedroom. But usually, without wasting any time, Father would go with these people to a little village. There we had our hiding place, but we didn't talk about it to anyone."

It is very late when the two girls decide to go to sleep. They would still have so many things to share. So often they saw how the Lord helped them.

It is Sunday afternoon at the church. The morning service is followed by a modest picnic. And now the little singers are arriving. Edidia is delighted to see and hear them. There are about fifty children, with four teachers and Genovieva's brother, Teodor, who accompanies them on the piano. They all know the songs by heart.

After a good practice, a break is welcome. But it is a short one. There are still several things on the program. Genovieva raises her hand for silence.

"Now we are going to ask God for His help and protection. Then we'll go out. Try not to attract attention. The *Securitate* is everywhere. We'll need about twenty minutes to get to the hospital. A sister from our church has been there for several weeks. Let's pray that our songs would encourage her and do good to the other patients. And pray that no one stops us."

A little later, disciplined and quiet, the whole team enters the entrance hall of the hospital. It is visiting time…

Suddenly young, clear voices fill the hall. What a surprise! Doors open everywhere, from both sides of the long corridor. What lovely songs and voices! All the patients want to hear them.

"What are you doing here?" asks a nurse on duty.

She doesn't seem happy with the words of these songs!

With a beautiful smile, Genovieva answers, "We have a friend in one of these rooms. We can't all get in. So it's our way of paying her a little visit."

When Edidia gets to the station after this nice day, her heart is overflowing with joy. What an encouragement for her new work with children! She hopes to meet Genovieva again. But will that ever happen? Where? How? When? Who knows?

Eventful Nights

Abruptly, Edidia is awakened from her sleep. That gentle knocking. Was it a dream? No... There is no doubt, someone is still knocking at the door.

Edidia looks at her watch. It is one o'clock in the morning. She goes into her parents' bedroom to awaken her father. The bed is empty.

Oh, yes, that's right. He is working this night. So I'll awaken Mother.

Quickly her mother gets up. She can hear the knocking at the door.

"Who's there?" she asks in a low voice.

"Pace!" a voice answers quietly.

The key turns, the door opens and two girls from abroad come in.

"We have Bibles," they say with an English accent. "A thousand! They are in our minibus at the end of the road."

"A thousand Bibles! What a treasure! Let me think where we could put this precious load. If only my husband were here... Right now he is driving the locomotive. Let's see... Listen, bring your car here, but drive without lights, so you don't attract attention. I will open the gate of our yard. Once you get in, I'll shut it after you. Then we can unload quickly."

Soon a chain of five people forms in silence. The parcels are passed from hand to hand from the minibus to the upstairs bedroom.

"God be with you," say the two courageous Christians, when all the Bibles are in the house.

Then they get back into their minibus.

Soon the sound of the engine disappears into the night.

Next morning Edidia's father comes back to see the bedroom full of parcels.

"Fantastic!" he exclaims. "But where shall we put all these Bibles? If only we had a car. What a pity I wasn't here! We could have gone with their vehicle straight to the hiding place. How shall we get them there, twenty miles away? I know... I'll phone Pavel, our Christian friend from Oradea. I'm sure he will help us with this transport. But I'll have to be very brief. The telephone lines are tapped. We could be discovered...

"Hello, Pavel! Come as soon as possible! A thousand..."

"I'll be right along."

That's all the two friends said. Then Pavel talks to his wife:

"They received a thousand Bibles! Great! I must go and help them to take them to a safe place."

"A thousand Bibles! That's wonderful! But one car is not enough. Let's ask Laura, our neighbor. I'm sure she would agree to follow you in her car."

"We must talk to her..."

How foolish! This Laura often comes to Christian meetings, it's true. But why? To learn from the Bible or to spy?

A thousand Bibles... Quickly Laura informs the secret services. Then she goes with Pavel in her car.

The following night 250 Bibles are loaded into each of the vehicles. They leave the town. But they do not get far. For no apparent reason the police stop them at a checkpoint. The Bibles are discovered. The load is seized. All that Pavel manages to do is to phone Edidia's father.

"We have nothing left," he says then hangs up.

"Let's not waste a minute," says Edidia's father. "We must save the other five hundred Bibles. Let's hide them in the piano, as many as will go in. The rest must be put in bags and taken out of the house as quickly as possible. Mihai will come immediately with his van to take them away. That brother knows how to get by."

A few hours later that night, Mihai's vehicle stops beside a river twenty miles away.

Edidia's father rolls up his trousers, gets hold of a bag and crosses the river. Mihai does the same, followed by Edidia, who has knotted her skirt above her knees.

Soon all the bags are on the other bank. In the darkness, they count them… One is missing! They grope around to look for it until they find it. Now comes the final stage.

The twelve bags are at last near the hiding place. In spite of the darkness, can you see those dark silhouettes, like a row of little houses? They are beehives. Some of them are empty. That will be useful. Their covers are raised, and soon the Word of God takes the place of the bees and their honey.

When the sun rises the bees start to buzz everywhere. Who would dare to come and look inside those hives? No danger there!

But late that morning the door of Edidia's house is shaken by violent knocking. Four agents from the *Securitate* are there.

"We have a search warrant!" is all they say for explanation.

And the search begins systematically.

"What is this black piece of furniture?" one of the inspectors suddenly asks.

Without knowing it, he points towards the rest of the Bibles.

"It's an old piano," replies Edidia calmly, and goes to put her trembling fingers on the keys. "It makes music, as you see… but it's a little bit dull."

76

The explanation seems to satisfy the policeman. A little later, having failed to find anything, they go away persuaded that nothing has escaped their severe search. What a relief for the whole family!

But there will be more surprise visits…

A few weeks later at three o'clock in the morning, in the night from Saturday to Sunday, someone again knocks gently at the door. Quickly they get up and ask who it is before turning the key.

A reassuring *"Pace!"* dispels all fear. They can open the gate.

Four girls are there. They have just come from the train station after twelve hours of traveling.

"Genovieva!" exclaims Edidia, recognizing her good friend. "What a surprise!"

"How are you, Edidia? As you see, I have come with three co-workers. Excuse me for not telling you we were coming. But we decided at the last moment. And, as you know, it's better not to write or speak on the phone. It is the best way to avoid having problems with the *Securitate*. I'm so happy to be in your home at last, Edidia! You know, God continues to bless us with the children. Perhaps we can talk about this work in your church. But first of all… would you have a little corner on the floor? We four weary travelers need to stretch out and sleep for a few hours."

What a joy! For such visits in Romania, you don't mind waking up, even in the middle of the night.

These Christians girls will spend that beautiful summer Sunday together. And what an unforgettable day it will be!

The Interrogation

When Delia leaves home, her school bag is heavy on her back. It's not that the little girl doesn't like to learn. On the contrary. She is a very good pupil. But since the other evening, she has been afraid. After what happened… will there be consequences? In spite of her fears, Delia quickens her step. She certainly mustn't get there late, or she could have more problems…

Lord Jesus, please help me! she repeats along the way.

Soon she sees the school building. Before going through the gate, Delia checks her uniform.

Quickly she arranges the ribbon which she wears on her head.

Instinctively, her fingers check that the number on the sleeve of her uniform is in place. It is there. So is the red scarf around her neck. All is in order. Her uniform is correct, according to the rules. Delia need not fear any reprimand.

Two teachers are on duty at the gate. They inspect each pupil that passes for his number and scarf, and the girls are checked for their ribbons as well.

Once through the control, Delia makes her way to her class of thirty pupils.

The bell rings. In silence, standing at their desks, the children watch for the teacher to arrive. There she is! But this morning, they are in for a surprise. The teacher is accompanied by the headmaster. Everyone is afraid of that man. Another teacher comes in as well, followed by a policeman. His boots and the revolver at his side make quite an impression. The children are alarmed. Why all these people?

At a signal from the teacher, everyone sits down with their hands behind their backs. Secretly Delia prays:

Lord Jesus, help me!

Suddenly the girl jumps as if awakened from a dream. Her name! Yes, she has just heard her name, Ionescu Delia, called by the headmaster! Already everyone is staring at her.

"Comrade Ionescu, come here!"

Very pale, Delia makes her way to the front.

"What did you do on Friday?" asks the headmaster dryly. "Where did you go? Answer!"

The whole class is stunned with shock. You could hear a pin drop.

Overcome with fear, her head down, the child remains silent… She can't even move her lips. She is trembling.

Everything flashes through her head like lightning. Yes, on Friday evening, she had gone to her Sunday school teacher's house with two friends she had invited. They were shown some slides. And they were told a story about Jesus. Suddenly the door was flung open. It was the police! They confiscated everything, the slides and the projector. But the worst thing was that they took the names of everyone there.

Since then, Delia has been afraid, especially of school.

Now… paralyzed by fear, and keeping her head down, she hears the headmaster's steps going to and fro in front of all the pupils. They too are terrified.

Now the policeman speaks:

"Your classmate Ionescu is a Christian. She is part of that group who don't respect the laws of the State or the Party. They are lazy, dangerous people. They are always trying to influence others. You should never listen to them or go with them. Otherwise you will have to answer to me. Understood?"

78

The teacher throws the cold water on the child's face. After a moment Delia revives.

She is very surprised to see her classmates all around her. They all seem terrified. But Delia is peaceful and has color in her cheeks. She even has a smile on her face.

"You know what?" says Delia. "I dreamed of the Lord Jesus! He was right here, in the classroom! He gave me a garland of flowers. He was so beautiful... and He smiled at me!"

Embarrassed, the children and the teacher don't know what to say. After what happened, everyone is sad. There is only one child who is smiling, and that is Delia.

This is a true story. It happened a few years ago. Delia belonged to a children's choir which was born in another town in Romania, after a visit from the Sion Choir which Genovieva started.

To sing for God could be very costly in Romania, even for a child. But the Lord Jesus promised always to be with those who belong to Him, even to the end of the world. He kept his promise for little Delia, the only Christian in her class.

What an example Delia is for us! Don't you think so, you who read these lines? Let's not be ashamed of believing the Bible. Let's not be afraid of being mocked. Jesus Christ was not ashamed of going to the cross for us. Let's believe in Him and live for Him. This is the way we can become courageous Christians and be useful to those around us.

Now it is the headmaster who speaks:

"Whom did you take with you the other evening, Comrade Ionescu? Come on! Answer me!"

Silence.

But, as white as a sheet, Delia keeps quiet. Then the headmaster seizes her by her hair, and shakes her furiously several times. Then, with brute force, he pushes her away.

The little girl falls heavily on the floor. She lies there motionless...

The headmaster, the policeman and the other teacher leave the classroom, slamming the door behind them.

The thirty pupils look with horror at their comrade lying there very pale, her eyes closed, motionless. She has fainted.

"Ana and Raluca!" the teacher says. "Give me a hand! We will lay her here on this bench. And you, Vali, go and get me a glass of water."

The Choir is Threatened

It is autumn. This Sunday, as every week, the members of the Sion Choir are rehearsing for the program. This evening they will sing in the church.

But there is a problem…

"I've just received bad news," says Genovieva. "I'm telling you so that we can all pray together."

No one says a word.

"This evening, we are going to have a visit from a high State official—a lawyer from Bucharest. He is well known to certain churches in the country. While the Christians were meeting, he arrived unannounced and interrupted the preaching of the Gospel. He had the churches closed down and the door sealed. No one knows for how long. This lawyer brings new regulations to restrict our choir activities. Besides, this is not the first time he has tried to stop us.

"What can we do?" continues Genovieva. "We have often seen God answering our prayers, so let's all tell Him about this new threat. He can do anything. Let's remember Saul of Tarsus who persecuted Christians. He was their worst enemy, but God made him their friend. The times are different. But the Lord is just the same. Why don't we pray that this man will be touched by our songs to the point of tears?"

The evening program will begin in a few hours. But before appearing in front of the congregation, the choir know they must come before God. Each one speaks to Him.

"Lord, bless this lawyer! Change him into a friend!"

"Lord, may he be touched by our songs even to the point of tears, as Genovieva said."

It is time to begin. The church hall is packed. Every seat is taken. People are standing everywhere—at the back, in the aisles and even in the entrance.

What about the lawyer? There he is, quite a tall man, well dressed, sitting in the front row. Having taken their places on the platform, the children have a good look at him. He has a broad face, lively features, and a mouth which seems incapable of smiling...

After the pastor's introduction, the choir stands up and begins to sing.

What freshness and life in their voices!

These children believe the words they are singing. You can feel it.

Now and again, between two songs, a little boy or girl recites a psalm. During this time the others can sit down and rest their voices. Then their singing continues even more beautifully.

From their place on the platform, the children take quick looks at the lawyer. He is sitting just opposite them, his face expressionless. If his mouth cannot smile, then his eyes probably cannot cry either...

The young people and children in the choir take a lot of trouble to articulate their words. A song is on their lips—but in their hearts they are praying to Almighty God.

While she is directing the choir, Genovieva sometimes wonders what is going on behind her back. Every time they get to the end of a song, she praises God in her heart because they were able to sing all the verses without interruption.

It is the end of the program. Suddenly the lawyer gets up...

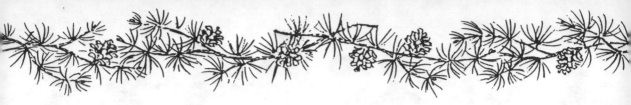

Everyone holds his breath. Is he coming up to speak? No! Just as he came in, the man leaves without a word.

The children are almost disappointed. Not even the smallest tear could be seen on the face of this powerful official!

"But… we prayed!" whispers a child in the choir to the one next to him.

"Yes, but… perhaps we went too far in our requests to God!"

Tears or no tears, what does it matter? The lawyer left. He made no threats. He didn't forbid anything. What a relief!

But God has in reserve a little surprise for all the members of the choir.

One week later, the children and young people are again on the platform ready to sing. Then a Christian from Bucharest, who is visiting Genovieva's church, asks to give a short message.

"I bring greetings to your church," he says, "and especially to the Sion Choir. From whom? From a lawyer in Bucharest. The one who was here last week. I met him when he returned from your church. When he told me of what he had seen and heard, he had tears in his eyes. This is what he told me, 'Those children… they sing so well and pray all the time! That *really* touched me!'"

At that all the members of the choir shout for joy. Spontaneously, they begin to clap. From now on everyone knows that God gives to those who ask. And when we are specific in our prayer, God is specific in His answer.

The Telephone Call

This evening some believers are having a meeting in secret. They are Christians known for their courage. Genovieva is there. So is Silvia. She is the girl who accompanies the choir so well on her guitar.

"There are more and more restrictions being placed on our activities. No longer allowed to do this... forbidden to do that. We must react. But how?"

"What the authorities fear most is that our situation should be known in the West."

"Well, let's write a letter defending the rights of Christians in Romania. Let's get a few signatures. And let's send a copy to our government!"

This is a bold move. But after praying, the believers make up their mind, and go ahead with it.

Reaction is not slow in coming. Like each of the other signatories, Genovieva receives a notice from the police. Immediately she has to go to the police station in her district.

"You are accused of signing a letter against the State," she hears. "We have to interrogate you. You should be at the *Securitate* headquarters tomorrow morning at eight o'clock."

What is going to happen? This could mean up to twenty years in prison, for each of the courageous signatories.

But this evening, Genovieva is at home with her family and several Christian friends. Together they are in prayer to God. Didn't they do this for the benefit of all believers? And isn't God almighty and able to protect His people?

The next morning she must go. Accompanied by her brother, Genovieva leaves the house...

"Look, we are here!" her brother says, nodding discreetly at an imposing three-story building. It is the *Securitate* headquarters for the town and the whole county. One wonders what goes on behind the curtains of those narrow windows?

For an hour already, Genovieva has been alone in an underground office. She is being questioned by a policeman who writes down everything she says. Then a second policeman comes in. He replaces the first one. He starts again from the beginning. But, unlike the first one, this man raises his voice and shows himself aggressive, even violent. Later a third one will come... It will go on like this until eight o'clock that evening. No one cares to give Genovieva anything to drink or eat. The poor girl is exhausted.

"We'll stop here!" she hears at last. "Go home and be here tomorrow at eight o'clock!"

Silvia has just been through the same thing. The two friends meet again at Genovieva's parents' house. They don't care for food. They would rather talk about what they have undergone.

Suddenly Silvia turns towards one of her friends.

"Victor, keep this telephone number carefully," she says to him. "It is my friends' number in England. Call them as soon as possible. The free world must certainly know what is happening here."

Victor goes very pale.

"You know, Silvia, most telephone conversations are listened to by the secret police. It could mean serious trouble for me. I don't know yet how I am going to do it, but I'll try. All right, you can count on me."

The next day the interrogations continue for Genovieva, with still more detectives...

Early in the morning Victor makes up his mind.

I'm taking great risks calling England, but the fate of several friends is at stake. I must do everything I can to help them.

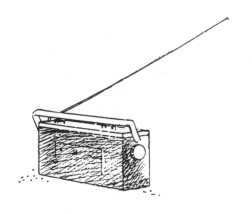

Wisely Victor avoids phoning from his home. When he lifts the receiver, everything is prepared. He has a text in English, with a list of names—the Christians who are under arrest and being submitted to these endless interrogations.

Slowly, he dials the number... It rings in England. They pick it up. Victor reads his text as quickly as possible, but he takes the time to spell each name on the list... He also specifies that some of these believers have been beaten.

The same evening, as usual, Victor turns on the radio to listen to an English broadcast for Romania. What does he hear all of a sudden? No, it can't be... So soon after his phone call? Yes, it is his message: "In the northeast of the country, several Christians have been arrested for writing a manifesto denouncing the limitations on their freedom. They have been subjected to long interrogations." Then he hears the list of names, just as he gave it a few hours before. Poor Victor! He panics. From now on, he too can expect to be arrested at any moment.

86

Next morning Genovieva is back at the secret police headquarters. The interrogations start again. But this time she finds the policemen nervous and visibly upset.

"Who told them abroad what is going on here?" they ask directly.

"That's for you to find out," Genovieva replies calmly. "I was here with you all day long."

What is going to happen to these courageous Christians in the hands of the secret police? Will they be shut away for long months behind the dark walls of a prison? No, because public opinion in the West has been alerted.

It is an evening in March. Genovieva has just arrived home. She is worn out after one more day at the *Securitate*. Tomorrow the interrogations will continue.

It is nine o'clock. At this very moment, in the basement of that sinister building, Christians are being beaten. But suddenly a muffled noise is heard, and curious shakings rock the whole town. It is an earthquake!

The damage is great, and hundreds of people die.

Running in all directions in panic, the policemen decide to free all the Christians under arrest.

What about Victor? He will never be troubled. Somehow his telephone call escaped being detected.

Victor, in fact, is not his real name. But, because he is still living in that town, it is wise not to reveal his true identity.

A Life in Danger!

"There is too much talk about your daughter," says a security agent to Genovieva's father. "Tell her to come at once to the office of the chief of the *Securitate*."

Then the policeman adds confidentially: "The best thing she can do would be to leave Romania. You are her father. It is up to you to convince her!"

Certainly, Genovieva's activities are causing too much of a stir. It is a country where the authorities do not want anything to do with God. These Christian songs for children and traveling with the choir have to stop!

Genovieva is now in the office of the chief of the *Securitate*.

"It is in your interest to leave Romania," he tells her dryly. "And you would do well to pay close attention to what I am telling you."

"What do you expect me to do?" sighs Genovieva.

"Write a petition at once!" replies the officer.

Genovieva thinks about it. *Leave?... but where shall I go?* she wonders. *I have no relatives abroad. I don't want to leave my family. Neither do they want to see me leave the country. And what about the children's choir and my friends?... They will feel so disappointed to see me leave! They will feel abandoned.*

But after this "advice" from the *Securitate*, Genovieva can only think: *Their suggestion is very smart. If I ignore it, I risk being put in a labor camp. Better to be far away, but in a free country. All right, it is decided!*

At the *Securitate* headquarters, Genovieva writes a petition. But wisely she puts it this way: "I request the right to work as a caretaker in my church, or if that is not possible, to leave the country."

The weeks stretch into months. Genovieva doesn't hear anything more about it. So she faithfully continues her work with the children.

The choir grows even more.

Those who are spying on it become exasperated. If we were to listen in on a certain office of the secret police, we would hear something like this:

"This Genovieva is getting on our nerves. She is causing trouble all over the country. We must get rid of her! But how?"

"Let's study the case carefully. Let's watch her comings and goings. Then we can put into operation a secret but effective plan!"

One January morning two people are walking quickly along a quiet road. In spite of the biting cold, Genovieva and her brother Costică have been to visit some friends. There they met several believers who are in danger. The brother and sister were the first to leave. At that hour there is not much going on; however, there is a car parked a little further down the road. The two young Christians take no notice of it.

Genovieva and Costică have walked about a hundred yards, when the engine of the vehicle starts up.

They soon arrive at the intersection. Now they are going to cross the road. The car drives forward, then stops. One of the three occupants makes a friendly sign to the two pedestrians to cross. They make a thankful sign in return, and start to cross the road...

Then, suddenly, the engine races, the tires squeal and the car drives forward, straight into Genovieva.

Aware of the danger, Costică seizes his sister by the arm and pulls her towards him. The vehicle brushes them, but no one is hurt.

Now the car brakes and comes to a stop.

"That's a *Securitate* vehicle!" exclaims Costică, seeing the number plate.

The plainclothes officers appear very surprised. They open the car window…

Costică reacts quickly.

"You wanted to kill my sister!" he shouts. "Why?"

But the policemen pretend not to hear. They close the window; then the car starts up and quickly disappears.

It was a very well-calculated blow, but it did not succeed. However, there is no doubt that Genovieva was the target. Her life is in danger. All she can do is put her trust in God, remembering this verse: "The name of the Lord is a strong tower. The righteous run to it and are safe" (Proverbs 18:10). Genovieva's family know how to lay hold of God's promises. They know the secret of prayer, too. But that doesn't mean they don't need to be very careful.

It is evening, and Genovieva is already lying down on her bench in the church. It is not yet late, but suddenly she hears someone shouting…

Quickly she understands. It is certainly not someone friendly towards the believers.

"We are going to close their church! We are going to close it! They will have to stop singing!"

Genovieva gets up, her heart beating fast. She carefully draws aside a curtain. She sees a car parked right in front of the gate.

It's them again! she sighs. *Lord, protect me!*

Finally the vehicle disappears, and calm returns. Wonderful!

But just before midnight the door is shaken by vigorous blows. Quickly Genovieva gets up. She is all alone. Should she open the door? Certainly not!

The knocking stops. But now… they are trying to force the door open. Genovieva climbs on a bench, gently opens a window, then gets up on the sill—ready to jump through the moment the door gives way… Now!

She jumps outside. And, like a cat, she manages to climb over the gate. Then she runs to some Christians who live nearby. From their house, she can see what is happening in the church. The policeman is taking out everything he can find: musical instruments, those used for the choir, the tape recorder, music sheets—everything goes out into the street!

How can we get rid of this person? By calling the police? That would be a waste of time!

Finally, one of the elders of the church is called, and he arrives on the scene. The secret policeman gives up and slips away. And that's the end of it.

But Genovieva is no longer safe. Will she make the big decision to leave her country? And will she be able to leave?

Corneliu's Present

"Genovieva, can you tell us a Christmas story? A true one from Romania. Please, Genovieva!"

"Just a minute. Let me think… Well, here's one, just as it happened."

The little town of Rădăuți was covered with fresh snow. That day, for once, the children really wanted to go to school. There were candles burning in the windows of the classroom, and smoke was rising from the chimney.

The children were sitting in their benches with their hands behind their backs. They were staring in amazement at the decorated "winter tree" in front of them. Under its branches there were many parcels.

The teacher, whom they called Comrade Rodica, was taking one parcel at a time, and each time she would read a new name on her list.

Glowing with pleasure, each child would get up to receive his present, then return to his place with a big smile.

In his seat at the back of the class, Corneliu was very excited. He came from a Christian family and this was his first year at school. He had never seen a decorated tree like that. Neither had he ever seen parcels wrapped in such pretty paper, tied up with ribbons. What could there be inside? Colored pencils? A game? Candy? A little toy? These were his dreams. Corneliu could hardly keep in his place. The giving of presents continued. There were just a few presents left, and one of them would be for him.

Three parcels left… then two… then one. That must be his! Corneliu was ready to dash up front. The teacher must be about to call his name. But another child was called and he got the last present! The little festivity was over, and school was over too.

Corneliu put up his hand, got up and said in a trembling voice, "Comrade Rodica, I didn't get anything. My name wasn't called!"

Immediately, all the children stopped looking at their presents. Their eyes turned in amazement towards the teacher and their classmate.

"I'm sorry, Corneliu," the teacher replied, "but for children who believe in God, there is no present! You can all go home!"

Corneliu put on his hat and his worn-out coat. He wrapped his scarf around his neck, and put on his boots.

Then, with a heavy heart, he ran home. "No gift for me! No gift for me!" he cried all the way, his boots leaving marks in the snow.

When he got home, his mother held him very tight. The child would not remain without something. Quickly she found a little surprise for him. Then she said:

"There is somewhere a present waiting for you, Corneliu… A big present. But you have to wait just a little. The Lord Jesus Himself will bring it to you, when He comes. It will be a crown. What a reward! But remember this: God loved you so much that He has already given you the greatest gift. He has given you His Son, Jesus, to become your Savior. Nobody could stop you from receiving that present. And nobody will ever be able to take it away from you."

Corneliu understood. Then he smiled. When he went to sleep, he was happy and proud to possess the most beautiful present of all.

What about you? Have you received this gift? All others are nothing in comparison with this one!

Ada in the Rain

Today Genovieva has a long talk with Ada. She is an old Christian lady, but just as active as she was fifty years ago. How many times this country woman has been helped by God! You could listen to her for hours when she starts telling stories from her life. Among her many adventures, there is one that Genovieva will never forget:

One day, Ada walks past the last houses in the village and takes a country road. After walking for half an hour she reaches the main road.

Lord, she prays silently, *You know there is no train or bus that stops here, but I am going to wait on the side of the road. Please make a car stop for me. I'll wait here...*

From time to time a car passes by. Ada holds out her arm, but nobody seems to take any notice. She has been waiting for an hour now by the side of the road.

The weather is cold and wet. Soon raindrops begin to fall.

Really, Lord! You could stop a car for me. I know You can... Just speak the word. Why don't You?

The rain gets heavier now. Poor Ada has no shelter. Her scarf, her coat, even her feet are all wet.

The time goes by... It rains even harder. Ada begins to cry. Tears mix with raindrops on her face. She has been waiting now for three hours.

Is it really worth going on waiting? Should Ada give up? But it is not for her own sake that she set out. She promised to go and visit someone in distress. Shouldn't she keep her promise at any cost?

There! The sound of an engine... In the distance a vehicle emerges at the bend in the road. Ada sees it and hopes once again, but...

No, it's no use getting too excited. It is a bus. Why would it stop here, in the middle of the country? But it seems to be slowing down... Yes, it is! It's coming over to the right. The driver lowers his window.

"Come, get on quickly!"

"Oh, thank you! How amazing! Thank you, thank you, Sir," shouts Ada, getting in at the back door and taking a seat on the last bench. "Thank you again!"

But who is that sitting right in the front of the bus? A little boy of ten or eleven. As soon as he hears Ada's voice, he turns around with an expression of amazement. *I know that voice,* he says to himself. And his face lights up in a big smile.

"Yes, it's her," he shouts, jumping up from his seat.

The child rushes into the aisle and runs towards Ada. He puts his arms around her neck and gives her a kiss.

Ada seems surprised. Who is this little boy?

"Don't you remember me? My name is Lionel. You told me about Jesus and you gave me…"

The child stops short and searches in his jacket pocket.

"…This!" he adds proudly, producing a Christian booklet which Ada knows well. "You know what, Miss? I accepted Jesus into my life. I am His child now. And I prayed for one whole year to see you again!"

Ada cries for joy.

Thank You, thank You, Lord! she prays spontaneously. *Oh yes, thank You for Lionel! It was worth waiting in the rain for such a reward. Thank You for stopping the right vehicle just for me—and for Lionel too!*

You Have to Leave!

A man has just got out of a black car, carrying a briefcase under his arm. He pushes open a small latticed gate, takes a few steps and knocks at the door of a small house.

Who lives there, at the end of this unpaved road? Genovieva's family.

The door opens.

"Security police! I want to see a girl by the name of Genovieva."

"…She's not here at the moment," her mother answers, trying not to show her anxiety.

"Do you know where I can reach her?" the man adds at once.

"Yes, she must be at the church, busy cleaning. She works there as a caretaker."

"I know! Well, send for her!" says the policeman, putting his briefcase on the table. "While I wait for her to come, I also want to ask you a few questions."

What has this man come for? To interrogate Genovieva again? Or perhaps to arrest her? On Sunday evening the children sang. The church was full. Was there a spy? What could he have told them? She has to be ready for anything.

Holding back a sigh, Mother turns to little Corina.

"Please, dear, go quickly and get Genovieva. She is at the church. Tell her that a gentleman from the police is waiting for her here. She must come at once!"

Corina runs off. She is a little nine-year-old who was abandoned. She was adopted by this already large family.

When she arrives at the church, the little girl rushes to open the door.

"Genovieva! Genovieva!"

"I'm here! What's up?" answers her big sister.

"Come quickly, Genovieva! There is a man at home. He came by car. He is someone from the *Securitate*. He wants to see you. He told us to get you, and that he would wait. Come quickly!"

Lord! You know everything. Please protect me!

Hand in hand, Corina and Genovieva hurry home. They don't say anything. *Another interrogation!* thinks Genovieva nervously. *But what else do they want to know? Lord, help me! Give me wisdom to answer all their questions.*

Out of breath and anxious, Genovieva pushes open the door of her family home. What does she see? The back of a stranger sitting at the table. Documents are spread out in front of him. He turns round, and Genovieva recognizes the face…

"We have already met," she hears. "I am the director of the visa and passport service. Remember, two years ago you made a petition to go to the United States. Later on I called you to my office. You wrote another petition, at my dictation. I am bringing you the answer…"

From his briefcase the officer takes an official document.

"The authorities are being very kind to you in giving you this passport!"

But what he adds comes like the sentence in a court:

"You have twenty-seven days to leave the country!"

What an act of kindness!

Genovieva's activities have so exasperated the *Securitate*, that they are in a hurry to get rid of her. *At last the children will stop singing,* they think. But how very wrong they are!

The officer left. He shut the door behind him.

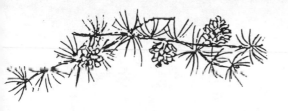

His car drove off. But the passport remained there. Genovieva quickly opens it.

"December!" she exclaims, looking at the date of issue. "So it has been ready for two months."

But another date stands out in big letters, with this sad statement: "Last day of exit from the country." Without a word, Genovieva shows the passport to her mother. Filled with emotion, they throw themselves into each other's arms. There are tears of joy and sadness. Far from her dear Romania, Genovieva will be safe. But at what a price! She has to leave her family, her friends and all the children... Oh, how hard that will be for her!

"There is no time to waste!" she says. "I have to get things moving at once with the American Consulate. As long as the answer doesn't take too long…"

Things are arranged very quickly. Genovieva will be received by the United States as a political refugee. She will have to fly to Rome. There, she will be taken care of by the American Embassy.

No problem getting to Bucharest by train, Genovieva realizes. *But where do I get the money for the ticket from Bucharest to Rome? I have an idea. Some doctor friends of mine gave me a nice cassette recorder for my work with the choir. I won't need it any more. I am going to sell it. That will cover a small part of the expenses.*

The cassette player is sold. But two days later the new owners bring it back to Genovieva.

"We heard that you had to leave. We want to give you 'our' cassette recorder back, so that you can sell it a second time!"

The news of her imminent departure spreads very quickly in the town. Then suddenly Genovieva finds herself having a lot of visitors. Many Christians come to say farewell to her. Each one of them wants to contribute, even just a little, towards the expense of the long journey.

"We want to come with you to Bucharest," say several children.

"And so do we," say many friends.

Finally Genovieva has enough money to pay for the trip. She will even be able to buy tickets for some of the children who will "escort" her to the airport.

March 16 is a farewell evening at the church for its dear "caretaker." The elders have put together a special program. But alas! The men from the *Securitate* are not slow to react.

"You can have this evening to say good-bye to your friend. But be sure of one thing. If anyone thanks her publicly, talks about her or her activities, he will have to settle accounts with us the next day!"

They will have to be content with a handshake at the door…

When the evening comes, the hall fills up long ahead of time. The doors are opened. Those who have to stand outside will still be able to hear.

At least five hundred people are there to say good-bye to their great friend.

All Alone
for the Journey?

The night train for Bucharest moves off. All the handkerchiefs are waving.

"La revedere! La revedere!" ("Good-bye! Good-bye!") shout all those left on the platform.

From the window of the car, Genovieva waves for a long time...

The train disappears into the night. She will never be able to forget this Wednesday, March 19.

An important page turns over in her life. At dawn the next day she will be in Bucharest. And on Friday morning she will fly to Rome.

Above her is a suitcase. And in her pocket is a passport, with the famous date by which she has to leave the country. In her heart she feels what anyone would feel when leaving for the unknown. Will she ever see her town again? Will she ever meet those who are so dear to her again? No one can say. One thing she knows is that she is leaving her dear Romania because she cannot continue to live there.

The next day will be very full. In Bucharest, Genovieva will have to contact the American Embassy, then go to the travel agency to confirm her reservation on the plane. Then she will see several friends.

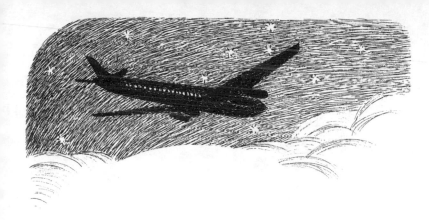

But, this evening she is in the train. Alone? No, she is not alone. Her God is very near to her. She knows that. He never leaves those who belong to Him. He promised. And in the Bible, Genovieva underlines this verse from chapter 54 of Isaiah: "Though the mountains be removed, yet My unfailing love for you will not be shaken, nor My covenant of peace be removed, says the Lord who has compassion on you." Right now the mountains of beautiful Moldavia are being removed. But God keeps His promise. He even made it possible for her to have many traveling companions. Everywhere in this car she is surrounded by friendly faces—those of her dear family, and many others too. One hundred and twenty people took the same train to the capital, to be with her until the hour of departure.

"But where are you all going to stay tomorrow night?" asks Genovieva, concerned.

"Don't worry about us!" her friends reply. "We will get by. But we want to be with you till the last moment."

On Friday morning the cold drizzle gives Bucharest a rather sad appearance. But they are at the airport on time, all waiting in the international departure hall.

The passengers have to be there two hours before the flight. They have to check their bags and confirm their seats.

"Who are all these people?" asks a policeman, turning to Genovieva. "Can I see your identity card?"

"Here is my passport. These are all my friends who wanted to come to say good-bye to me."

"Wait a moment!"

The policeman talks to a colleague.

"To have such an escort this traveler must be a personality. Who is she?"

"Call the *Securitate*. They will certainly be able to inform us."

Suddenly the policeman comes back towards Genovieva.

"Will you come with me, please!"

So she follows this officer, thinking she will come back in a few minutes.

She goes through the checkpoint They stamp her passport. But afterwards, she cannot go back! There she is in the waiting hall all by herself, two hours before departure. She is so near to her friends, but it is impossible to see them again!

Then they make her get on the plane. She will stay there a long time alone, surrounded by empty seats...

Emotions at the Airport

"The plane for Rome is at the end of the runway. And to think that Genovieva is inside it…"

"And we couldn't even say good-bye to her!"

Suddenly the jet engines begin to rev up. The plane accelerates on the runway, gets up speed… and takes off.

From her window, Genovieva tries to catch a glimpse of the city. But the plane is already over the countryside. It gains altitude and shudders as it goes through a ceiling of clouds… Now it is in the sunshine. The landscape is magnificent. White clouds stretch into the distance like endless mountains and valleys.

Genovieva is leaving for the unknown. There are no relatives to surround her, and no friends to encourage her. But God is there, very near to her. *Remember, My child,* He says to her heart, *when*

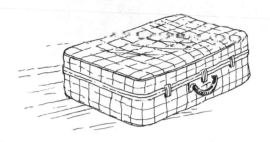

the mountains are removed... I will never leave you Count on Me!

Then, as verse 5 of Psalm 37 tells her, Genovieva commits her way to the Lord. She puts all her trust in Him. She knows that He will take care of her.

In the narrow aisle of the plane, the staff get busy.

"This is for you, Madam," says a friendly stewardess, holding out a meal on a tray.

"...No, thank you!" replies Genovieva.

At that moment, she couldn't really eat anything. She prefers to snuggle into her seat and shut her eyes. That way she can better think of those so abruptly left behind.

Did she doze off? In any case, Genovieva is very surprised to hear over the loudspeaker: "In ten minutes we will be landing in Rome?"

"Already?" she exclaims.

Many thoughts then pass through her mind. She quickly remembers: *Oh, yes, that's right. They will be waiting for me. Only yesterday the American Embassy in Bucharest assured me, "Everything is in order. We have just sent a telegram to our colleagues in Rome. After you go through the passport control, you will see someone carrying a sign with your name on it. Introduce yourself. They will help you."*

The plane comes to a stop. A gangway is put in place. The arriving passengers are led to the entrance of the airport terminal. They come into a big hall. A conveyer belt starts moving. It will deliver the luggage to the passengers...

Each one in turn takes hold of his suitcase or bag, puts it onto a trolley, then disappears into the crowd.

Genovieva waits. Her suitcase still hasn't come. Little by little the number of travelers around her diminishes. Here comes a little red suitcase, followed by a big box. A man grabs them impatiently...

There are no more bags on the conveyer belt. It stops.

Only one person is still waiting. It is Genovieva. That suitcase contains all that she possesses. And her precious luggage is not there! She must report it quickly. Genovieva goes to a counter.

"Prego: cosa desidera?"

They speak Italian here. But airport staff know English.

"Leave us your address," they tell her. "As soon as your suitcase is found, we will let you know."

"My address? ...I only have the American Embassy. Besides, they are supposed to meet me here. I will quickly go and see, then come back..."

Genovieva looks all around. Where is that sign with her name? At that other exit? No one there either!

But how can that be? sighs the Romanian girl. *They promised me that someone would be here...*

So what is going on? The explanation is very simple. As a final "friendly" gesture, those who hated Genovieva so much made sure that the telegram never arrived in Rome, and that the suitcase was left in a corner of Bucharest airport!

So no one is waiting for Genovieva. She is all alone in foreign airport, in a country where she doesn't speak the language, without her suitcase, and with no Italian money to buy even a piece of bread!

In the airport director's office, Genovieva explains her situation in English.

"We will do everything we can to help you," she hears gratefully.

They telephone the American Embassy. The answer is very clear.

"We know indeed that this person is to arrive in Rome, but we are still waiting for details by telegram... What do you say? She is there? But we were not informed! Then we will come to get her. Tell her that we are coming... All right, in your office."

Genovieva is reassured. But she will need a lot of patience. Rome is a big city, and there is a lot of traffic. Poor Genovieva! She has to wait three long hours...

At last an official from the American Embassy arrives. Finally the Romanian girl is taken care of. She is safe now. She gets into a comfortable car, and is taken to a hotel. But it is more than twelve hours since she had breakfast before leaving Bucharest. Since then she has had nothing to eat. And no one realizes that she could be hungry or thirsty. Arriving passengers have had a good meal on the plane. Oh, how much she will appreciate a meal the next day!

Like all "refugees" in their care, Genovieva will stay there for ten days before continuing her journey. And on the tenth day she will get her suitcase back!

At last she takes off for New York. The mountains of Moldavia are even further away now, but God's faithfulness is just the same. Exactly as He promised!

A New Mission

"Can I help you, Madam?" asks a nice airport hostess.

She is talking to a mother with two children.

We are in New York, in the arrival terminal of the airport. Who is this devoted hostess? Did you guess? It is Genovieva!

Genovieva arrived in New York a few months before, and was warmly received as a refugee. She was welcomed with an envelope containing a hundred dollars for her immediate needs.

"I must go and look for a job at once!" she had said before leaving her family.

But a big surprise was waiting for her when she got off the plane.

"Oh… you speak English very well!" the person in charge of her realized right away. "We could give you a job here at the airport, if you are interested. You would be responsible for welcoming and helping people needing assistance."

That is how her life began in the United States.

Oh, what a change for Genovieva! She doesn't need to stand in endless lines for bread any more.

She doesn't need to hide in a church for fear of the police. No more threats, no more hardship, no more shivering because of the lack of warm clothes.

The first time she went into a supermarket, she was astounded. When she saw those full shopping carts, she thought of the Romanian housewives who go home with empty bags after hours of waiting outside the shops.

In the United States there is no need to hide Bibles and distribute them in secret. What a joy for Genovieva to attend Christian meetings in perfect freedom!

"No more problems for you, Genovieva!" they tell her. "Now make the most of your freedom, enjoy life, and try to forget the years of hardship."

"No, I cannot do that," she replies. "Here I have everything, but there in my country thousands of children continue to shiver in winter, and many believers are still persecuted. When I think of them, I feel I am suffocating in my new comfort."

Lord, she prays earnestly, *in my homeland I worked for You. But here… what is my life good for? Show me what I can do. I so much want my life to be useful to You!*

The answer is not slow in coming…

"Tell me, Genovieva!" a Christian friend soon asks her, "would you mind if we arrange a meeting in the church?"

"A meeting… what for?"

"You could tell us about your country, about Christians in Romania, and their needs…"

"If it is to share the burden for my dear country, of course I would be glad to!"

So the evening meeting is announced. And suddenly the congregation have their eyes opened to the sad realities of Romania. Someone has a question.

"How could we help?"

"I promised…" answers Genovieva rather hesitantly, "I promised to do all I could to send a sweater to each child in the choir in Iași. Those children are so poor, you know…"

"Well, let's have a collection at once!"

On the spot 750 dollars are received for the sweaters. Genovieva is so happy!

"You are expected in another church," she soon hears. "You should speak about the same things. The Christians here must know about Romania."

Invitations increase, and so do the gifts. She has to open an account for all the money.

"Genovieva, you should start a mission to help Romania," suggest several friends.

"I already thought of that," she replies. "And I even prayed for it. What you say encourages me to go ahead with it."

Look at this storehouse! It is Genovieva's bedroom! She lives in the little space not taken up by stocks of food. When she prepares the care parcels, the storehouse looks like a post office.

Once a month, friends come and load the parcels into their car. Then everything gets mailed. How happy Genovieva is with each new shipment! She doesn't realize that soon thousands of parcels will be sent from the United States to Romania.

The work grows. There are many invitations. Saturday in one town, the next day in another. Genovieva has never traveled so much. Finally she has to give up all other activities. But the Mission to help Romania is born.

In her homeland, Genovieva learned to be content with little. She knew what it meant to be hungry. Now she has plenty. But she continues to think of those who lack everything. She is really happy. Why? What is her secret? The answer is found in the first verse of Psalm 41: "Blessed is he who is concerned for the poor."

Have we learned how to share? Let us learn to think of others. We will quickly discover that the more one gives, the more one receives.

Stephen and Genovieva

Congratulations!

"Look, the door is opening!"
"They are coming out…"
"Yes, there they are…"
"Oh, how beautiful she is in that long white dress!"
"Congratulations!"

At this time of the year, the sun often forgets to shine on that little town in England. But today, Saturday, November 16, 1985, joy fills their hearts. Stephen and Genovieva are getting married! Congratulations!

Genovieva's mother, who has been a widow for several years, is present. She is the only guest from Romania. Some friends have come from the United States. But the congregation is composed mainly of English people who know Stephen, the young teacher. He taught French for two years in this little town, southwest of London.

The wedding ceremony has just finished. The couple wanted an English wedding. But, from the beginning to the end, they remained standing, as in Romania. When the time came to sign the marriage certificate, they went into another room for about ten minutes.

While they were away, suddenly a hundred children could be heard singing in the church. What marvelous songs! People couldn't understand the Romanian words, but they certainly felt the conviction and warmth in their voices.

Have a hundred children really come from Romania? Is that possible? Yes, but not exactly the way you think…

For these children the celebration started a month earlier—in Romania, in the church in Iași, in the very place where Genovieva had to hide for so long. They sang with all their heart for their great friend's wedding. She certainly deserved it. Someone recorded their voices on a cassette and mailed it… Miraculously it arrived! It was to be expected that these children should have a part in the ceremony. Their choir was born when Genovieva lived in Iași, among them.

"Genovieva we know well," you will perhaps say. "But who is Stephen? It is the first time we meet him in this long story."

"The first time? Really? No! Remember? It was dark when we saw him at work, in secret…"

It was in Iași, one evening, when three foreigners gave poor Genovieva a fright without wanting to. They had gone to the church where she was hiding. She took them for officers of the *Securitate*. How frightened she was!

But soon she heard in English, "Hello! Are you Genovieva? I am Stephen, and these are my two friends. We are Christians from England. We are just passing through your town and someone gave us the address of this church. We are bringing you forty Bibles. Where can we leave them?"

How exciting for Genovieva! Hadn't she given her Bible that very afternoon to a courageous Christian forcibly held in a psychiatric hospital? In order to encourage this person with the Word of God, Genovieva had given away her most precious treasure. And that very evening, she was to receive forty Bibles! God was at work on her behalf, and also on behalf of these three young men who had taken great risks.

That night, before taking to the road again, they had stayed with Genovieva's parents. Then they had gone on their way.

Stephen lived in England. His parents had been missionaries in Morocco. At the age of fourteen, he decided to follow the Lord.

While at school, he liked foreign languages the best.

One day Stephen made a suggestion to two of his friends:

"How about taking a trip into Eastern Europe during our next vacation? We have often prayed for the Christians over there. What a joy if we could take some help to Romania, Bulgaria, or even the Soviet Union!"

The three young men made serious preparations and set off in a car. But it was a long journey. What adventures they had! They also faced difficulties which could easily have discouraged them. However, one evening they arrived in Iași with their forty Bibles. Oh, what a joy! And what memories, too!

Afterwards, Stephen became a French teacher. He went back to Eastern Europe several times after that. Later, he worked in Austria for four years, in a mission for Romania, Turkey and other countries.

One day, whom does he meet? Genovieva! In the United States she had published several books for Romanian children. She was looking for a way to get them into Romania. There was only one mission that was able to help. So Genovieva took a trip to Austria to make contact with them. And what did she discover? That was where Stephen was working! They met and got to know each other better.

God had prepared them for each other. He brought them together. Then, after a period of time… they were married.

How is the Lord going to use this couple in His service? Where will He lead them?

Back to the Homeland

"Good evening, little friends in Romania! We are glad you can be with us again for our program *Walking with God*. Together, we are going to discover wonderful things in the Bible. But first of all, here is a beautiful song for you. It comes from Switzerland. Its title is *Who created the world?* The children sing so joyfully! Let's listen to them..."

Who is at the microphone making this announcement? Genovieva! She has been going regularly to a recording studio to make radio programs.

We are now in a little town in Germany. Stephen and Genovieva have moved there to be nearer to Romania. Genovieva would love to return there to tell the children about the Bible. But it's still forbidden to believe in God! School children are still forced to repeat: "God does not exist, God does not exist!"

In Romania Genovieva would again risk being put in prison. She cannot go back there.

"But then, what can we do to tell these children that God does exist, and that He loves them?"

That's the question Stephen and Genovieva have often asked themselves. They have always come to the same conclusion.

"We must get into the country. But how?"

God will show them the way. It has to be a way that will allow them to cross the borders without a passport and go anywhere—a way to enter many homes without being seen. This way is radio.

Now, each Monday evening, Genovieva has a quarter of an hour to speak to thousands of Romanian children.

They are hungry, they are cold, they live in fear, but they are happy to be able to listen to this broadcast in secret. What a joy to meet with their friend again on the air every Monday!

Listeners write:

"We record your programs for the Sunday school. This way we can teach our children these beautiful songs."

"Dear Genovieva, on Monday mornings I am often beaten at school because on Sundays I go to church with my parents. But do you know what always encourages me? Your program, which comes on Mondays. We listen to it as a family, quietly, of course, because of the neighbors. And when we hear 'Till next time…' we all say, 'Already?' But we all look forward to the next Monday. Please don't mention this letter on the radio. It could create more problems for us."

Besides preparing radio programs, Stephen and Genovieva make food parcels of flour, sugar, powdered milk, rice, coffee and medicines. Every month from 60 to 70 parcels, each weighing over 40 pounds, are taken to the post office.

Then, more letters arrive:
"When I received your parcel, I wept for joy. I gave praises to God. Thank you for everything! I was able to exchange the coffee for wood for the stove…"

Stephen and Genovieva also publish books for the Romanian children. Beautifully illustrated by a Christian artist, they tell the stories of Christmas, Easter and Creation. Thousands of copies find their way to Romania. And later on all sorts of beautiful cassettes for children will replace the radio broadcasts.

It is Christmas 1989. The whole country is shaken by incredible events. It is the revolution, resulting in the fall of the terrible and cruel dictator! At last the Christians will be able to meet without fear. What a joy!

A little later, Stephen and his wife go to Romania for a few weeks.

They are in Iași. On that little road that goes uphill, on the right, there is a gate, then some steps... It is in this building that Genovieva had to hide for so long. How excited she is when she sees again the benches in her church!

What a celebration there is on Sunday when in that same place she meets so many friends!

"Do you remember this Bible, Genovieva? You hid it one day under some paper at the bottom of a dustbin so that I could have it."

"Genovieva! Do you recognize me? I was a member of the choir. I was with you when they tried to push us off the bus that evening in the middle of the forest."

"Genovieva! Do you want to show your husband the hill where the storm saved us from those who were following us? I would love to take you both there in my car tomorrow."

There are still many things that need to change in this country. But the Christians are so happy now to meet together, to sing, and to open the Bible in perfect freedom!

Songs sung by the original Sion Choir from Iași were recorded while Genovieva was still in Romania. A cassette of these songs in Romanian, as well as additional copies of this book, can be ordered from the following address:

Eastern Europe Aid Association
P.O. Box 917
Waynesboro, PA 17268-0917, U.S.A.

Cassette cover: the Sion Choir in 1978, while touring churches in Bucharest. On the right, facing the choir, is Genovieva, and playing the organ is Teodor, her brother.

Children's songs
sung in Romanian by the
Sion Choir
from Iași (Romania)